Our Roots
Black History Sketchbook

TAYO FATUNLA
with a foreword by ROLAND RAMPAT

"TO FOLUSO TOYO and JOLA"

Copyright©2004. Text and Contents - TAYO Fatunla 2004.
All rights reserved. A CIP catalogue record for this book is
available from the British Library.   ISBN 0-9539357-1-X
No part of this compilation may be reproduced, stored in a
retrieval system, or transmitted, in any form or by any means
without the prior permission in writing of the Author, nor be otherwise
circulated in any form of binding or cover other than that in which it is published
and without a similar condition including this condition being imposed
on the subsequent purchaser. Folta Limited, P.O. Box 240, Dartford Kent DA1 3WY, England

Attention: Schools and Businesses
Posters of all sizes of the illustrations in this book and more are available at your request.
Please write and email to tfatunla@hotmail.com

Printed in Great Britain

The Pride in Black Roots - ROLAND RAMPAT

It was indeed a privilege to be asked by the famous cartoonist and illustrator TAYO Fatunla to pen the foreword for his compilation of OUR ROOTS.

Those of us familiar with OUR ROOTS know only too well the depth of passion and energy with which TAYO approaches his research on his subjects, all expressed vividly in his very own style and presented in considerable detail in his cartoon illustrations.

TAYO uses cartoons and illustrations to relate and communicate to the world and educate it about the achievements of both present and past black heroes who have made a significant impact on both our way of life and the world we live in today.

Look at the fundamental contribution to the world of classical music made by the great virtuoso Ludwig Van Beethoven. He was a black composer of partly African origin. Not many people are aware of this information. Very little is mentioned about the remarkable contributions of black women to our rich culture such as the first black James Bond girl, Gloria Hendry or the Ashanti Kingdom's warrior queen, Yaa Asantewa. They are role models for our generation of today. Furthermore, and even more significant is the arrival of the MV *Empire Windrush* in 1948 to Britain, bringing the first wave of Caribbean immigrants who have since made an impact on the British culture. All these significant landmarks are fully documented in this absorbing illustrated history of the achievements of black people, their past, present and future.

OUR ROOTS documents various stages in the history of the Black race and is easy to read. It is an educational enhancement in anyone's library.

I surely can identify with the MV *Empire Windrush*, as my roots arrived in Guyana, formerly British Guiana, in 1900 as indentured immigrants from India.

OUR ROOTS is fun to read and comes highly recommended. TAYO is pleased with the impact OUR ROOTS has made and I am too.

ABORIGINES

WILLIAM LANNEY WAS ONE OF THE LAST TASMANIAN **ABORIGINES**. LANNEY SUFFERED GREAT INDIGNITY IN LIFE AND IN DEATH AT THE HANDS OF WHITE SETTLERS. IN THE 1830S THERE WERE ABOUT 13,000 ABORIGINAL INHABITANTS OF TASMANIA. THE **ABORIGINES** WERE FISHERS AND FOOD GATHERERS. THEY LIVED TOGETHER IN SMALL BANDS AND MOVED FROM PLACE TO PLACE FOR SURVIVAL. THE WORD **ABORIGINES** COMES FROM THE LATIN **ABORIGINE**, MEANING FROM THE BEGINNING.

TAYO FATUNLA

TOM ADAMS

TOM ADAMS (1931-1985) WAS PRIME MINISTER OF BARBADOS FROM 1976 TO 1985. ADAMS WAS ELECTED LEADER OF THE OPPOSITION, THE BARBADOS LABOUR PARTY, IN 1971 HE PROVED HIMSELF A WORTHY LEADER OF HIS WEST INDIAN ISLAND. **ADAMS** WAS DEVOTED TO HIS ISLAND AND ITS PEOPLE, POLITICALLY AND ECONOMICALLY. **ADAMS** WAS A STRONG AND COMPASSIONATE LEADER. ON THE INTERNATIONAL SCENE, **TOM ADAMS** WILL BE REMEMBERED FOR HIS PARTICIPATION IN THE CONTROVERSIAL UNITED STATES INVASION OF GRENADA.

AFFONSO I

AFFONSO I (DATE OF BIRTH UNKNOWN) ASSUMED THE THRONE OF THE KING OF CONGO IN WEST CENTRAL AFRICA AFTER THE DEATH OF HIS FATHER IN 1506. HE HAD A MUCH MORE ACTIVE RELATIONSHIP WITH THE PORTUGUESE THAN HIS FATHER BUT THIS RELATIONSHIP DETERIORATED BECAUSE HE REQUESTED A TIGHTER CONTROL ON THE PORTUGUESE NATIONALS WHO WERE MORE INTERESTED IN THE SLAVE TRADE THAN THE EXCHANGE OF THEIR SERVICES FOR CONGO'S HANDICRAFTS. AND ALSO BECAUSE OF **AFFONSO'S** CONCERN FOR HIS ROYAL AUTHORITY WHICH LED TO INCREASING DISRUPTION BY THE PORTUGUESE. AN ATTEMPT WAS MADE ON **AFFONSO'S** LIFE IN 1540 BY EIGHT PORTUGUESE WHO PLOTTED TO SHOOT HIM IN A CHURCH ON EASTER DAY. THIS MARKED THE END OF HIS REIGN. **AFFONSO I** RULED AS KING OF CONGO FROM 1506 TO 1543. **AFFONSO'S** REIGN LEFT LASTING MEMORIES IN AFRICA AND EUROPE.

TAYO FATUNLA

WINDRUSH ARRIVANTS

ON JUNE 22 1948, THE M.V. **WINDRUSH** DOCKED AT TILBURY AND CHANGED THE FACE OF BRITISH HISTORY FOREVER WITH THE FIRST MASS BLACK MIGRATION TO BRITAIN. THE SHIP CARRIED THE FIRST WAVE OF CARIBBEAN MIGRANTS WHO WERE LOOKING FOR A FRESH START IN BRITAIN. THE GROUP OF **WINDRUSH ARRIVANTS** NUMBERED 492 AND INCLUDED MOSTLY MEN AND A FEW WOMEN AND ONE CHILD, A THIRTEEN YEAR OLD BOY. SINCE THEN, THE BLACK COMMUNITY HAS MADE A REMARKABLE IMPACT ON THE BRITISH CULTURE AND COMMUNITIES ARE RICHER FOR THE HERITAGE AND TRADITIONS THEY BROUGHT. IN 1998, THERE WERE SEVERAL CELEBRATIONS TO MARK THE 50TH ANNIVERSARY OF THE HISTORIC MIGRATION OF THE **WINDRUSH ARRIVANTS**.

YAA ASANTEWA

NANA (QUEEN) YAA **ASANTEWA** LED THE ASHANTIS INTO BATTLE AGAINST THE BRITISH. IT WAS BAD ENOUGH THAT THE BRITISH HAD INSULTED AND DEPORTED THE KING OF THE ASHANTI NATION TO THE SEYCHELLES ISLANDS IN 1896, BUT THEN THEY DEMANDED THE SURRENDER OF THEIR MOST SACRED POSSESSION, THE GOLDEN STOOL. THE ASHANTI NATION LOST THE WAR BUT **YAA ASANTEWA** IS REMEMBERED FOR HER BRAVE ATTEMPT TO SAVE HER NATION FROM HUMILIATION.

TAYO FATUNLA

DR. NNAMDI AZIKIWE WAS BORN IN 1906 AT ZUNGERU IN PRESENT DAY NIGER STATE IN NIGERIA.
HE STUDIED AND WORKED IN THE U.S. BETWEEN 1925 AND 1934. BETWEEN 1934 AND 1937, **ZIK** SETTLED IN GOLD COAST (NOW GHANA), WEST AFRICA, WHERE HE WAS EDITOR OF *THE AFRICAN MORNING POST*. **ZIK**, AS HE WAS POPULARLY KNOWN, WAS A LEADING JOURNALIST, NATIONALIST AND POLITICIAN IN THE GOVERNMENT, AND THEN BECAME GOVERNOR-GENERAL. WHEN NIGERIA BECAME A REPUBLIC IN 1963 **ZIK** BECAME ITS FIRST PRESIDENT. **DR. NNAMDI AZIKIWE** WAS LOVED BY NIGERIANS AS A MAN OF VISION AND HUMANITY. THE LATE ELDER STATESMAN AND LEADER OF THE IGBOS FROM EASTERN NIGERIA DIED IN 1996.

NNAMDI AZIKIWE

The singing star and energetic performer **Josephine Baker** (1906-1975) was a poor African-American girl who became an international star and established herself as a symbol of sexuality. **Baker** made her Broadway debut in the chorus line of *Shuffle Along* in 1923 and she began singing in Harlem's Plantation Club before moving to France. **Baker** used her celebrity status to speak against discrimination. The darling of France, **Baker** performed to the French jazz enthusiasts topless. She married a French Jew and was targeted by the Nazis. She toured the U.S., South America, Europe and the Far East, but stayed mainly in France with a "Rainbow Tribe" of adopted children from many countries. **Josephine Baker** addressed the crowds at the 1963 Civil Rights March on Washington.

JOSEPHINE BAKER

TAYO FATUNLA

JOSEPHINE BAKHITA

Mother **Josephine Bakhita** was born in Sudan, North-East Africa in 1869. Mother **Bakhita** experienced the humiliations and suffering of slavery before being taken to Italy by an Italian Consul. She received the Sacraments of Christian Initiation became a nun with the Canossian Order, taking her vows in 1890 and with each day, became more aware of God whom she felt she knew and loved. Mother **Bakhita** comforted the poor and suffering. She spent many years of her life as a witness to faith, goodness and Christian hope. Mother **Josephine Bakhita** was loved by many Italians. She was canonised by the Catholic Church in the year 2000.

TAYO FATUNLA

BALEGA MASK

The **Balega Mask** is from the **Balega** tribe who live to the northwest of Lake Tanganyika in the Congo (Democratic Republic). Unlike other traditional masks, the **Balega Mask** is not made for wear on the face but worn on the arm to signify the passage of a member of the Bwami Society, from one grade to another. The Bwami Society dominate the Balega community

TAYO FATUNLA

12

SLAVE BARRACKS

TO PREVENT SLAVES ESCAPING WHILE AWAITING TRANSPORTATION, **SLAVE BARRACKS** (FROM THE 17TH CENTURY) WERE BUILT ON THE SLAVE COASTS OF WEST AFRICA. THESE SLAVES WERE KEPT IN TERRIBLE CONDITIONS AND EXPOSED TO THE ELEMENTS, GUARDED BY THEIR FELLOW AFRICANS. THEIR LEGS WERE USUALLY TIED TO HEAVY LOGS OF WOOD AND THEIR HANDS TIED TOGETHER. THEY WERE USUALLY SOLD TO EUROPEAN SLAVE CAPTAINS WHO BOUGHT THE SLAVES IN EXCHANGE FOR RUM, BRANDY (TO INTOXICATE THE AFRICAN TRADERS), COTTON GOODS, IRON BARS AND GLASS BEADS.

TAYO FATUNLA

NORMAN BEATON

NORMAN BEATON (1934-1994) WAS BORN IN GUYANA. **BEATON** MOVED TO GREAT BRITAIN IN 1960 AND BECAME INVOLVED IN THE THEATRE AS A SINGER. HE BECAME A HOUSEHOLD NAME ON BRITISH TV, WITH A LARGE FOLLOWING AMONG BOTH BLACKS AND WHITES, IN THE LONG-RUNNING COMEDY *DESMONDS* SET IN PECKHAM, SOUTHEAST LONDON. **BEATON** ALSO APPEARED ON THE POPULAR AMERICAN SITCOM, THE *BILL COSBY SHOW*. IN 1977, **NORMAN BEATON** WAS THE FIRST BLACK ACTOR TO WIN THE VARIETY CLUB OF GREAT BRITAIN FOR BEST FILM ACTOR.

TAYO FATUNLA

MUHAMMADU BELLO

THE FIRST HOLDER OF THE TITLE OF SULTAN OF SOKOTO IN NORTHERN NIGERIA WAS **MUHAMMADU BELLO** (1781-1837). A SCHOLAR, THEOLOGIAN AND WRITER, THE SULTAN OF SOKOTO HAD SOVEREIGNTY OVER THE AREA CONQUERED BY HIS FATHER UTHMAN DAN FODIO'S ISLAMIC JIHAD (HOLY WAR). **SULTAN BELLO** WAS A LEADING COLLEAGUE OF HIS FATHER IN THE JIHAD. THERE WERE REVOLTS DURING **SULTAN BELLO**'S REIGN BUT THIS DID LITTLE TO STOP HIS REFORM OF THE KINGDOM. **SULTAN BELLO** WROTE MANY POEMS IN PRAISE OF PROPHET MUHAMMED AND THE JIHAD. HIS SCHOLARLY REPUTATION WAS NOTED BY THE BRITISH TRAVELLER CLAPPERTON IN THE 1820S.

TAYO FATUNLA

HALLE BERRY

IT HAD ELUDED A BLACK ACTRESS FOR SEVENTY FOUR YEARS BUT IN THE YEAR 2002 **HALLE BERRY** (1968-) MADE OSCAR HISTORY. SHE BECAME THE FIRST BLACK WOMAN TO WIN THE BEST ACTRESS AWARD FOR HER ROLE IN *MONSTER'S BALLS*.

BERRY WAS BORN IN CLEVELAND, OHIO AND STUDIED BROADCAST JOURNALISM AND LATER ON STUDIED ACTING IN CHICAGO. SHE GREW UP FACING MANY CHALLENGES INCLUDING CULTURAL DIFFERENCES DUE TO HER MIXED RACE ORIGINS. SHE WAS DETERMINED AND WHILE STUDYING ACTING, HER FIRST BIG IMPRESSION WAS ON THE SILVER SCREEN IN SPIKE LEE'S *JUNGLE FEVER*, STARRING OPPOSITE WESLEY SNIPES. NAMED AFTER THE DEPARTMENT STORE HALLE BROTHERS, **BERRY** HAS CREDITED SPIKE LEE FOR GIVING HER, HER MOVIE BREAK. **HALLE BERRY** HAS ALSO STARRED IN MOVIES WITH ACTORS SUCH AS JOHN TRAVOLTA, KURT RUSSELL, EDDIE MURPHY (*BOOMERANG* 1992) AND DANNY GLOVER.

TAYO FATUNLA

MAURICE BISHOP

MAURICE BISHOP (1944-1983) BEGAN HIS POLITICAL INVOLVEMENT IN GRENADA IN 1970, THE YEAR THE BLACK POWER MOVEMENT GAINED STRONG APPEAL IN THE CARIBBEAN ISLAND. **BISHOP** WAS LEADER OF THE JEWEL MOVEMENT. FIVE YEARS AFTER THE INDEPENDENCE OF GRENADA IN 1974, **BISHOP** TOOK OVER CONTROL OF THE GOVERNMENT OF GRENADA IN 1979 AND TRIED TO TRANSFORM THE SOCIETY ACCORDING TO THE CUBAN MODEL. **BISHOP** WAS AN ACTIVE PRIME MINISTER WHO DESPITE HIS GOVERNMENT'S ACHIEVEMENTS, HELD NO ELECTIONS. **MAURICE BISHOP** WAS KILLED IN A COUP IN 1983.

TAYO FATUNLA

BLACK PEOPLE IN NAZI GERMANY

IN ADDITION TO THE JEWS, GYPSIES AND OTHER ETHNIC MINORITIES IN NAZI CONCENTRATION CAMPS, THERE WERE ALSO BLACK GERMANS WHO WERE PERSECUTED BEFORE AND DURING WORLD WAR II. MANY WERE CHILDREN OF AFRICAN SOLDIERS (OF FRENCH OCCUPATION FORCES AFTER WORLD WAR I) AND GERMAN WOMEN; THEY WERE STERILIZED BY THE NAZIS' ORDER. DURING ADOLF HITLER'S REIGN OF TERROR, IN WHICH MORE THAN 8 MILLION INNOCENT PEOPLE WERE EXTERMINATED, THE BLACK GERMANS FOUGHT HARD AGAINST NAZISM. **LARI GILES** WAS MURDERED BY THE SS (THE NAZI POLICE WHO CARRIED OUT THE EXTERMINATION) FOR THE ROLE HE PLAYED IN LEADING A RESISTANCE GROUP WHO FOUGHT THE NAZI IN HIS HOMETOWN OF DUSSELDORF.

TAYO FATUNLA

DAVID BLAINE

DAVID BLAINE (1973-) WAS BORN IN BROOKLYN, NEW YORK AND RAISED BY HIS MOTHER ALONE. THE YOUNG, FAMOUS AND ECCENTRIC MAGICIAN'S FIRST EFFECT WAS PASSING A CIGARETTE THROUGH A CARD BOUGHT FOR HIM AT THE DISNEY MAGIC SHOP IN FLORIDA. HE HAD AN AMBITION TO BECOME A MASTER MAGICIAN. BLAINE IS THE FIRST MAGICIAN TO USE HIS PERFORMANCES TO CUT THROUGH ALL CULTURAL BARRIERS. HE TOOK HIS MAGIC TO THE STREETS OF NEW YORK, HAITI AND SOUTH AMERICA. HIS FIRST SPECIAL "*DAVID BLAINE: STREET MAGIC*" AIRED IN 1997. IT WAS AN INSTANT SUCCESS. HIS SECOND SPECIAL, "*DAVID BLAINE: MAGIC MAN*" WAS AIRED ON TELEVISION IN 1999. AMONG DAVID BLAINE'S MAGICAL FEATS WERE BEING FROZEN IN A BLOCK OF SOLID ICE IN NEW YORK, STANDING ON A PLINTH FOR 33 HOURS AND SUSPENDED IN A GLASS BOX IN LONDON FOR 44 DAYS WITHOUT FOOD.

TAYO FATUNLA

PAUL BOGLE

Leader and organizer, the Right Excellent **Paul Bogle**, national hero of Jamaica was hanged in 1865 for leading the *Morant Bay Rebellion*, suppressed by the British who killed hundreds, while a great number were flogged and punished. **Bogle**, who lived in St. Thomas, stood up for people's rights. A reward of two thousand pounds was offered for his capture. **Paul Bogle** was caught near Torrington on 24 October 1865 and hanged. The rising led to widespread condemnation of Governor Eyre, responsible for the repression and the imposition of direct rule from London.

TAYO FATUNLA

BARBARA BRANDON

BARBARA BRANDON (1958-) IS THE FIRST BLACK FEMALE CARTOONIST TO BE SYNDICATED IN THE MAIN STREAM PRESS. BORN IN BROOKLYN, NEW YORK, BRANDON STUDIED ILLUSTRATION AT SYRACUSE UNIVERSITY. SHE HAD HER FIRST COMIC STRIP IN THE FREE PRESS IN 1989 CALLED *WHERE I AM COMING FROM*, AND THE UNIVERSAL PRESS SYNDICATE GAVE THE STRIP AND BRANDON A WIDER READERSHIP WHEN IT ACQUIRED IT IN 1991. THE STRIP WAS ORIGINALLY CREATED FOR *ELAN*, A BLACK MAGAZINE FOR WOMEN BUT THE MAGAZINE WENT OUT OF BUSINESS BEFORE THE STRIP WAS PUBLISHED. BARBARA BRANDON BASED HER POLITICAL COMIC STRIP ON NINE BLACK GIRLS WITH DIFFERENT LIFESTYLES AND VIEWS.

TAYO FATUNLA

JOANNE CAMPBELL

THE FIRST BLACK BRITISH ACTRESS TO PLAY SARAH IN *GUYS AND DOLLS* AND AMANDA IN *PRIVATE LIVES* WAS **JOANNE CAMPBELL** (1964-2002), ACTOR AND DRAMA THERAPIST WHO WAS BORN IN NORTHAMPTON, ENGLAND, BRITAIN. **CAMPBELL** TOOK AFTER HER PARENTS FROM WHOM SHE DERIVED HER ACTING ABILITY. SHE TRAINED AT THE ARTS EDUCATIONAL SCHOOL IN LONDON.

HER FIRST ROLE WAS THE HERO IN *JACK AND THE BEANSTALK* AT THE THEATRE ROYAL STRATFORD, LONDON IN 1982. **CAMPBELL** WAS A ROLE MODEL TO ASPIRING YOUNG BLACK BRITISH ACTORS. SHE PLAYED LIZ, THE SECRETARY IN THE POPULAR BRITISH SITCOM *ME AND MY GIRL*. **CAMPBELL** MADE VERY MANY T.V. APPEARANCES IN ENTERTAINMENT AND IN CHILDREN'S TELEVISION. SHE BROUGHT LIFE TO CHARACTERS SHE PLAYED INCLUDING HER ROLE AS JOSEPHINE BAKER IN *THIS IS MY DREAM*. **JOANNE CAMPBELL** WAS A CARING PERSON WHO IN THE MID-1990S TRAINED AS A DRAMA THERAPIST. HER WARM APPROACH ENABLED HER TO GAIN THE TRUST OF HER PATIENTS.

TAYO FATUNLA

JACOBUS CAPITEIN (1717-1747) WAS A BLACK DUTCH THEOLOGIAN OF AFRICAN DESCENT. **CAPITEIN** WAS SOLD AS A SLAVE AND TAKEN TO HOLLAND FROM AFRICA AND IT WAS WHILE IN HOLLAND HE STUDIED GREEK, HEBREW, CHALDEAN AND IN ADDITION THEOLOGY. HE BECAME A MASTER IN THEM. **CAPITEIN** PREACHED TO LARGE WHITE CONGREGATIONS WITH SUCCESS. HE RETURNED TO AFRICA IN 1742 TO SAVE HIS OWN PEOPLE WITH A NEW RELIGION. HIS PEOPLE REGARDED HIS RELIGION AS IDOLATRY AND WOULD HAVE NONE OF HIM. ONE OF **JACOBUS CAPITEIN'S** QUESTIONABLE BELIEFS WAS THAT SLAVERY COULD REDUCE IDLENESS.

JACOBUS CAPITEIN

TAYO FATUNLA

GEORGE WASHINGTON CARVER

GEORGE WASHINGTON CARVER (1860-1943) WAS ONE OF THE BEST KNOWN AGRICULTURAL SCIENTISTS OF ALL TIME. BORN IN MISSOURI, **CARVER** DIRECTED THE TUSKEGEE INSTITUTE'S AGRICULTURAL RESEARCH DEPARTMENT IN ALABAMA (USA), AND HE WAS ALSO OF GREAT ENCOURAGEMENT TO THE SOUTHERN AMERICAN FARMERS, BY USING HIS EXTENSIVE RESEARCH TO HELP THEM. **CARVER** NEVER PATENTED MANY OF HIS DISCOVERIES. IN 1948, **GEORGE WASHINGTON CARVER** WAS HONOURED BY A U.S. POSTAGE STAMP AUTHORIZED BY PRESIDENT TRUMAN.

KALPANA CHAWLA

THE FIRST ASIAN ASTRONAUT WOMAN IN SPACE, **KALPANA CHAWLA** WAS BORN IN 1961. BORN IN KARNAL, INDIA, **CHAWLA** MIGRATED TO THE U.S. WERE SHE LATER BECAME AN AMERICAN CITIZEN. HER FIRST FLIGHT WAS ON STS-87 IN 1997. SHE TOOK A B.SC IN AERONAUTICAL ENGINEERING FROM PUNJAB ENGINEERING COLLEGE IN 1982 AND LATER AT THE UNIVERSITY OF COLORADO. **CHAWLA** LOVED FLYING AEROBATICS. IT WAS NOT A SURPRISE THAT SHE WAS SELECTED FOR ASTRONAUT TRAINING IN 1994. HER FIRST FLIGHT WAS ON STS-87 IN 1997. **CHAWLA** WORKED ON TECHNICAL ISSUES OF SPACE WALKING AND ROBOTIC EQUIPMENT. ON RETURN FROM A SPACE MISSION, **KALPANA CHAWLA** AND SIX OTHER CREW MEMBERS INCLUDING AN AFRICAN-AMERICAN LOST THEIR LIVES AS THE SPACE SHUTTLE COLUMBIA DISINTEGRATED OVER TEXAS ON FEBRUARY 1 2003.

CHRIST THE REDEEMER

ONE OF THE MOST POPULAR TOURIST ATTRACTION IN RIO DE JANEIRO IN BRAZIL, IS THE STATUE OF **CHRIST THE REDEEMER** (CRISTO REDENTOR) WHICH STANDS ON TOP OF CORCOVADO MOUNTAIN (HUNCHBACK MOUNTAIN). STANDING THIRTY METRES TALL, THE STATUE IS THE ONE OF THE WORLD'S BEST-KNOWN AND MOST VISITED MONUMENTS. IT WAS ORIGINALLY CONCEIVED IN 1921 AND DEVELOPED BY ENGINEER HEITOR DA SILVA COSTA. THE STATUE REPRESENTS JESUS STANDING WITH OUTSTRETCHED WELCOMING ARMS. THE **CHRIST THE REDEEMER** STATUE ALSO BLESSES VISITORS AND RESIDENTS FROM ON HIGH.

TAYO FATUNLA

CELIA CRUZ (1925-2003) THE AFRO-CUBAN QUEEN OF MAMBO AND SALSA MUSIC, REPRESENTED THE EMERGING IDENTITY OF HISPANIC-AMERICA IN THE 1940S. **CRUZ** WAS BORN IN THE SANTA SUAREZ NEIGHBOURHOOD OF HAVANA, CUBA. SHE WAS THE ONLY WOMAN TO HAVE RETAINED THE STATUS OF LATIN AMERICA'S MOST WORSHIPPED SINGER. SHE BEGAN SINGING IN THE 1930S ON THE RADIO IN CUBA AND ALSO SANG AFRO-CUBAN YORUBA RELIGIOUS MUSIC. **CRUZ** SANG IN THE WORLD FAMOUS TROPICANA CASINO. SHE WAS ONE OF THE ARTISTS TO BREAK THAT CLUB'S PRE-REVOLUTIONARY COLOUR BAR. AFTER THE REVOLUTION OF 1959, SHE DEFECTED TO MEXICO WITH ONE OF CUBA'S LONGEST STANDING DANCE ORCHESTRA LA SONORA MATANCERA. FIDEL CASTRO WHO WAS A BIG FAN WAS DEVASTATED BY THE DEFECTION AND DID NOT FORGIVE **CELIA CRUZ**, WHO LATER LIVED IN THE UNITED STATES WHERE SHE DIED. SHE RECORDED MORE THAN SEVENTY ALBUMS.

CELIA CRUZ

PAUL CUFFEE

PAUL CUFFEE (1759-1817) BEGAN HIS CAREER AS A SAILOR AND WENT ON TO BECOME SUCCESSFUL IN THE SHIPPING BUSINESS. BY 1806, CUFFEE HAD OWNED THREE SHIPS, LAND AND MORE THAN ONE HOUSE. **CUFFEE** ENCOURAGED THE RESETTLING OF AFRICAN-AMERICANS IN AFRICA, AND TO ADVANCE THIS CAUSE HE LED A VOYAGE TO SIERRA LEONE IN 1815. LIKE MOST OF THE BACK-TO-AFRICA ENTHUSIASTS AT THE TIME SUCH AS RICHARD ALLEN AND JOHN RUSSWURM, **PAUL CUFFEE** SOUGHT TO USE HIS RESOURCES AND TALENTS TO BETTER THE LOT OF THE AFRICAN-AMERICANS WHO WERE SUFFERING UNDER SLAVERY.

TAYO FATUNLA

DINGANE

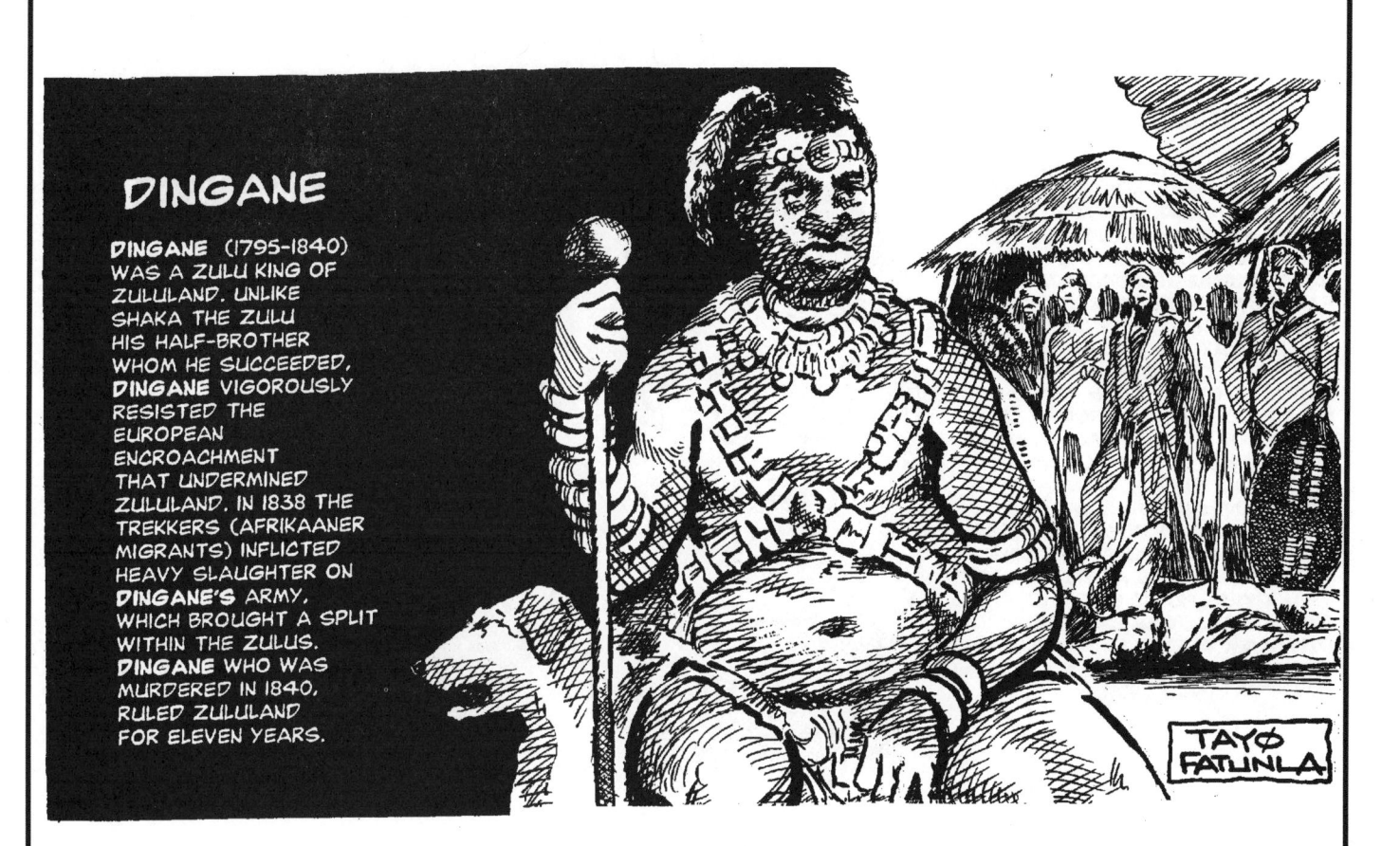

DINGANE (1795-1840) WAS A ZULU KING OF ZULULAND. UNLIKE SHAKA THE ZULU HIS HALF-BROTHER WHOM HE SUCCEEDED, **DINGANE** VIGOROUSLY RESISTED THE EUROPEAN ENCROACHMENT THAT UNDERMINED ZULULAND. IN 1838 THE TREKKERS (AFRIKAANER MIGRANTS) INFLICTED HEAVY SLAUGHTER ON **DINGANE'S** ARMY, WHICH BROUGHT A SPLIT WITHIN THE ZULUS. **DINGANE** WHO WAS MURDERED IN 1840, RULED ZULULAND FOR ELEVEN YEARS.

TAYO FATUNLA

JEAN-CLAUDE DUVALIER

PRESIDENT **JEAN-CLAUDE DUVALIER** OF HAITI (1951-) WAS WELL KNOWN AS "BABY DOC". **DUVALIER** SUCCEEDED HIS FATHER "PAPA DOC" FRANCOIS DUVALIER IN 1971 AS "PRESIDENT FOR LIFE" AT THE YOUNG AGE OF 19. **DUVALIER** WAS KNOWN FOR THE WRONG REASONS. HE RULED HAITI WITH AN IRON HAND USING THE "TONTON MACOUTES", **DUVALIER'S** SECRET POLICE. HIS REGIME DID NOT TOLERATE POLITICAL OPPOSITION, JUST LIKE HIS FATHER'S, AND EVENTUALLY, IN 1986, THERE WAS A POPULAR UPRISING THAT BROUGHT TO AN END THE 29-YEAR DYNASTIC RULE OF THE **DUVALIERS**. **JEAN-CLAUDE DUVALIER** AND HIS FAMILY FLED HAITI TO AVOID BEING KILLED OR ARRESTED.

BABY DOC! BABY DOC! BABY DOC!

TAYO FATUNLA

EMBALMING

THE PROCESS OF **EMBALMING** A DEAD BODY ORIGINATED FROM ANCIENT EGYPT IN NORTH AFRICA. THE WORD USED FOR THIS PROCESS IS MUMMIFICATION. IN THE **EMBALMER'S** WORKSHOP, THE ORGANS OF A DEAD PERSON WERE REMOVED AND PLACED IN SPECIAL CONTAINERS. THE BRAIN WAS EXTRACTED THROUGH THE NOSTRILS AND THE HEART WAS LEFT IN THE BODY. THE EMPTY BODY CAVITY AND SKULL WERE PACKED WITH PRESERVATIVES AND THEN WRAPPED UP WITH LONG LINEN BANDAGES. THIS **EMBALMING** PROCESS LASTED SEVENTY DAYS. THE EGYPTIANS CALLED THIS MUMMIFICATION PROCESS "AFTERLIFE."

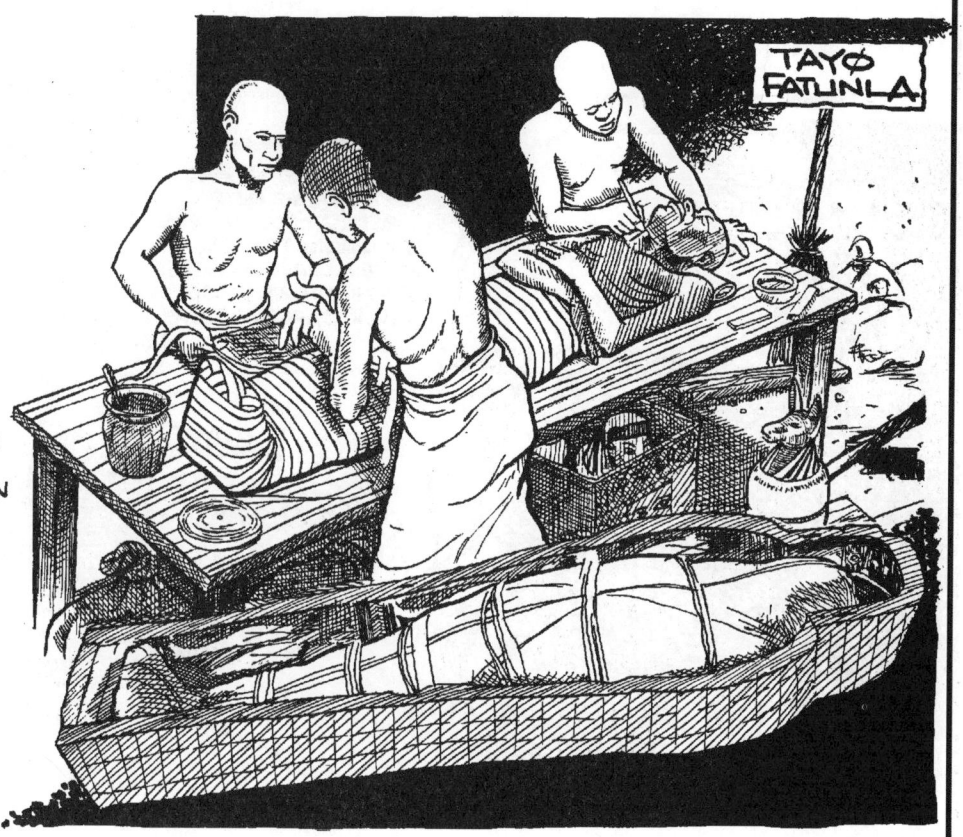

CARLOS FINLAY

CARLOS FINLAY WAS BORN IN 1833 IN CAMAGUEY PROVINCE IN CUBA. HE HAD A DEGREE OF THE UNIVERSITY OF HAVANA, BECOMING A PRACTICING MEDICAL DOCTOR. **FINLAY** SETTLED PERMANENTLY IN CUBA IN 1870 AFTER TRAVELLING TO PERU, TRINIDAD AND FRANCE WORKING IN VARIOUS HOSPITALS. HE DEVELOPED AN INTEREST IN CUBA'S SANITARY AND HEALTH PROBLEMS AND IN 1879, **FINLAY** DISCOVERED THAT CERTAIN MOSQUITOES TRANSMIT YELLOW FEVER. **CARLOS FINLAY** WORKED FOR THE CUBAN GOVERNMENT AS A PUBLIC HEALTH CHIEF. HE DIED IN 1915.

TAYO FATUNLA

ARETHA FRANKLIN

ARETHA FRANKLIN (1942-), KNOWN AS THE "QUEEN OF SOUL", BEGAN HER MUSICAL CAREER AS A GOSPEL SINGER AND THEN MOVED INTO THE MORE LUCRATIVE WORLD OF SOUL MUSIC. **FRANKLIN** MADE HER FIRST RECORD AT THE AGE OF TWELVE AND HER GREATEST SUCCESS CAME WITH THE SONG "RESPECT" WHICH STRUCK THE RIGHT CHORD WITH THE AFRICAN-AMERICAN CIVIL RIGHTS MOVEMENT IN THE 1960S. SHE ALSO SANG THE "RESPECT" SONG IN THE MOVIE *THE BLUES BROTHERS* IN WHICH SHE FEATURED. **ARETHA FRANKLIN** WAS BORN IN MEMPHIS, TENNESSEE. HER SINGING CAREER HAS YIELDED NUMEROUS AWARDS INCLUDING THE GRAMMYS.

TAYO FATUNLA

INDIRA GANDHI

She made history when she became the Prime Minister of the world's biggest democracy, India. Stateswoman **INDIRA GANDHI** (1917-1984) joined the Indian National Congress in 1938 and was elected president of the Congress in 1959. After her father's death in 1964, his successor Shastri appointed her to his government. Shastri died in 1966 and **GANDHI** became Prime Minister. **GANDHI** broke the electoral rules in the 1971 elections and refused to resign. Her party lost the 1977 elections but in 1980, she made a comeback as Prime Minister again. She was surrounded by men yet isolated. **INDIRA GANDHI** was assassinated by a Sikh extremists. She played a strong political role in the creation and governing of independent India.

AMY-JACQUES GARVEY WAS BORN IN 1896. SHE WORKED FOR THE FAMOUS JAMAICAN NATIONALIST, MARCUS GARVEY AS HIS SECRETARY AT THE UNIVERSAL NEGRO IMPROVEMENT ASSOCIATION (UNIA), IN THE U.S. AN ORGANISATION THAT TRIED TO BRING TOGETHER THE WORLD'S AFRICAN PEOPLES, THROUGH RACIAL PRIDE AND ECONOMIC POWER. **AMY-JACQUES** LATER BECAME MARCUS GARVEY'S WIFE. WHEN MARCUS GARVEY DIED IN 1940, **AMY-JACQUES** GARVEY REMAINED ACTIVE IN BLACK NATIONALIST WORK, WORKING HARD TO KEEP HER LATE HUSBAND'S MESSAGE ALIVE UNTIL HER DEATH IN 1973.

COTTON GIN

AMERICAN INVENTOR, ELI WHITNEY IN 1793, INVENTED THE **COTTON GIN** WHICH MADE IT POSSIBLE TO CLEAN THE GREEN SEEDS FROM THE MUCH HARDIER, SHORT-STAPLE BOLL WHICH WAS GROWN PROFITABLY THROUGHOUT THE SOUTHERN UNITED STATES BETWEEN 1790 AND 1810. THE **COTTON GIN** REPLACED THE LABOUR OF AT LEAST FOURTEEN PLANTATION SLAVES.

THERE WAS ALWAYS THE DIFFICULTY IN SEPARATING THE COTTON LINT FROM THE SEED WHICH WAS A SLOW AND VERY TROUBLESOME PROCESS. SEPARATION THEN WAS DONE WITH FINGERS. LARGER MACHINE-OPERATED VERSIONS OF THE **COTTON GIN** WERE INTRODUCED DURING THE 19TH CENTURY.

ELI WHITNEY'S ORIGINAL COTTON GIN

TAYO FATUNLA

BERNIE GRANT

BERNIE GRANT (1944-2000) WAS A HIGHLY RESPECTED BRITISH FIGURE WHO FACED HEAVY CRITICISM IN AND BEYOND POLITICAL CIRCLES. BORN IN GEORGETOWN, GUYANA, **GRANT** ARRIVED IN THE UNITED KINGDOM WITH HIS FAMILY IN 1963. **GRANT** WENT INTO BRITISH POLITICS SUPPORTING CONTROVERSIAL PROJECTS AND FIGHTING LOCAL CAUSES FOR BLACK BRITONS. HE WORKED HIS WAY UP THROUGH THE POLITICAL RANKS FROM BEING A COUNCILLOR TO BECOMING A LABOUR PARTY MEMBER OF PARLIAMENT (MP) FOR TOTTENHAM IN NORTH LONDON IN 1987. **BERNIE GRANT** WENT INTO PARLIAMENT WEARING AGBADA AND SOKOTO (AFRICAN ROBES).

CHE GUEVARA

ERNESTO "CHE" GUEVARA (1928-1967) WHO HAS BECOME AN ICON TO MANY TODAY, WAS ONE OF THE MOST POWERFUL MEMBERS OF THE CUBAN GOVERNMENT UNDER FIDEL CASTRO. **GUEVARA** WAS ASSOCIATED WITH REVOLUTIONARY MOVEMENTS THROUGHOUT LATIN AMERICA AND AFRICA, FROM THE CAPITALS OF HAVANA AND ALGIERS TO THE BATTLEGROUNDS OF BOLIVIA AND CONGO, WHERE SEVERAL REBELLIONS WERE INITIATED INVOKING THE RADICAL NAME OF PATRICE LUMUMBA. IN 1967 **CHE GUEVARA** WAS CAUGHT AND KILLED BY BOLIVIAN GOVERNMENT FORCES.

ADELAIDE HALL

A jazz innovator, African-American born **ADELAIDE HALL** (1904-1993) was one of Britain's best loved entertainers. She was a jazz innovator who made Britain her second home in 1938. She was often recognised by local residents while shopping in London's North End Road. Ms **Hall** performed with Duke Ellington, Art Tatum and Fats Waller. She also performed in Broadway, New York, in the West End musicals in London, at the Cotton Club in New York and in Chicago and Paris among other places. Ms. **Hall's** style was musical-comedy star. She joined an elite group of black entertainers in Britain and succeeded in breaking away from the blackface 'minstrel' image of people of African descent. In 1951, wherever she performed, **ADELAIDE HALL** was breaking box office records with record attendance. A film about her life and career entitled the *Sophisticated Lady* was commissioned for TV by a British television company. Her hit show songs include "I Must Have That Man" and "I Can't Give You Anything But Love".

TAYO FATUNLA

BRITON HAMMON

The Royal Naval College buildings in Greenwich part of which now houses part of the University of Greenwich, in South East London, were built as a hospital for seamen who were in their old age or sick or could no longer earn their living at sea. In 1694. It housed over 2,000 sailors from the Royal Navy. In 1759, the first black presence was that of Briton Hammon who was an inmate at the hospital. Hammon's autobiography Narrative of Briton Hammon was the first black person's life story to be seen in Britain. Hammon could not read or write so, he dictated his life history. Hammon served on both merchant and military ships and he spent six weeks in the Greenwich Hospital for Seamen.

Tayo Fatunla

40

OLIVER HARRINGTON

OLIVER "OLLIE" **HARRINGTON** WAS A CARTOONIST WHO USED HIS ARTISTRY, HUMOUR AND BITING WIT TO FIGHT AGAINST RACIAL INJUSTICES IN THE USA. **HARRINGTON**, KNOWN FOR HIS COMIC CHARACTER, "BOOTSIE" (1935), ATTENDED AN UNSEGREGATED SCHOOL IN THE SOUTH BRONX, NEW YORK WHERE A RACIST TEACHER WAS RESPONSIBLE FOR STARTING HIS CAREER AS A CARTOONIST. **HARRINGTON** MOVED TO EAST BERLIN WHERE HIS CARTOONS MADE HIM A FAVOURITE AMONG STUDENTS AND INTELLECTUALS. HE DIED IN GERMANY IN 1995 AT THE AGE OF 84 AFTER A 34-YEAR SELF-IMPOSED EXILE. **HARRINGTON** HAS BEEN DESCRIBED AS "AMERICA'S GREATEST BLACK CARTOONIST".

HE WAS KNOWN FOR HIS ELOQUENCE. **JAMES AUGUSTINE HEALY** (1830-1900) WAS THE FIRST BLACK CATHOLIC PRIEST AND BISHOP IN THE U.S. **HEALY** WAS BORN IN GEORGIA. HIS FATHER, A WHITE PLANTATION OWNER, WAS A WEALTHY IRISHMAN WHO DEFIED GEORGIA LAWS BY MARRYING A FREED SLAVE. **HEALY** WAS HIGHLY REGARDED AND WELL KNOWN WITHIN THE CATHOLIC COMMUNITY. **HEALY** SERVED AS A PASTOR AND THEN AS AN ADMINISTRATOR IN THE BOSTON ARCHDIOCESE BEFORE HE WAS APPOINTED AS THE BISHOP OF PORTLAND, MAINE IN 1875. HE OVERSAW THE BUILDING OF MANY CHURCHES. ORDAINED IN 1854, **JAMES HEALY** ENJOYED THE FRIENDSHIP OF POPE PIUS IX AND POPE LEO XIII.

FIRST!

JAMES HEALY

TAYO FATUNLA

GLORIA HENDRY (1949-) was the first Black "James Bond Girl" to feature in the 007 James Bond movie series. Born in Florida, **HENDRY** worked as a secretary in the New York office of the NAACP and was also a Playboy "Bunny" at one point in time. In the 1970s, Hendry starred in many popular African-American movies. Born in Jacksonville, Florida, **HENDRY** was raised in New Jersey. Her first exposure to acting was in the movie *For The Love of Ivy* in the James Bond movie, *Live and Let Die* (1973), **HENDRY** played a double-crossing CIA agent, Rosie Carver. She made history, though, by being the first romantically-involved African-American James Bond girl opposite British actor Roger Moore, who was the third James Bond in a line of various actors who have played the role of Agent 007. **GLORIA HENDRY** also starred in Black action movies such as *Black Caesar* and *Black Belt Jones*.

MOORE BOND
7"
"LIVE AND LET DIE"

GLORIA HENDRY

TAYO FATUNLA

IBAKA

IBAKA (1820-1889) WAS A WEALTHY CONGOLESE AFRICAN CHIEF WHO ENGAGED IN THE 19TH CENTURY CONGO (THE PRESENT DEMOCRATIC REPUBLIC OF CONGO) RIVER TRADE.

IBAKA WAS A LEADING ALLY OF EARLY EUROPEAN EXPLORERS AND MISSIONARIES WHO ESTABLISHED OUTPOSTS IN HIS TERRITORY. AS A CHIEF OF THE BOBANGI COLLECTION OF VILLAGES AT BOLOBO, IBAKA'S POWER DEVELOPED THROUGH HIS FRIENDSHIP WITH THE EUROPEANS. HE USED THE INFLUENCE GAINED IN COMMERCE TO INCREASE HIS POWER. WHEN IBAKA DIED, THE BOBANGI TRIBE SACRIFICED SEVEN TO EIGHT SLAVES TO ACCOMPANY HIM TO THE OTHER WORLD.

TAYO FATUNLA

DANIEL JAMES JR.

DANIEL "CHAPPIE" JAMES, JR. (1920-1978) WAS THE FIRST AFRICAN-AMERICAN FOUR STAR GENERAL IN THE UNITED STATES AIR FORCE NICK NAMED "BLACK PANTHER", **JAMES** COMMANDED 63,000 MEN. BORN IN PENSACOLA, FLORIDA, **JAMES** FLEW 179 MISSIONS IN THE KOREAN AND VIETNAM WARS. HE WAS AMONG THE BEST PILOTS IN AIR FORCE HISTORY WHO CARRIED OUT FEARLESS DEEDS OF HEROISM. HE WAS WIDELY AWARDED AND DECORATED IN AND OUT OF THE MILITARY. AT ONE TIME, **DANIEL JAMES JR.** CONTROLLED ALL AIR ATTACK FORCES IN THE U.S. AND CANADA.

TAYO FATUNLA

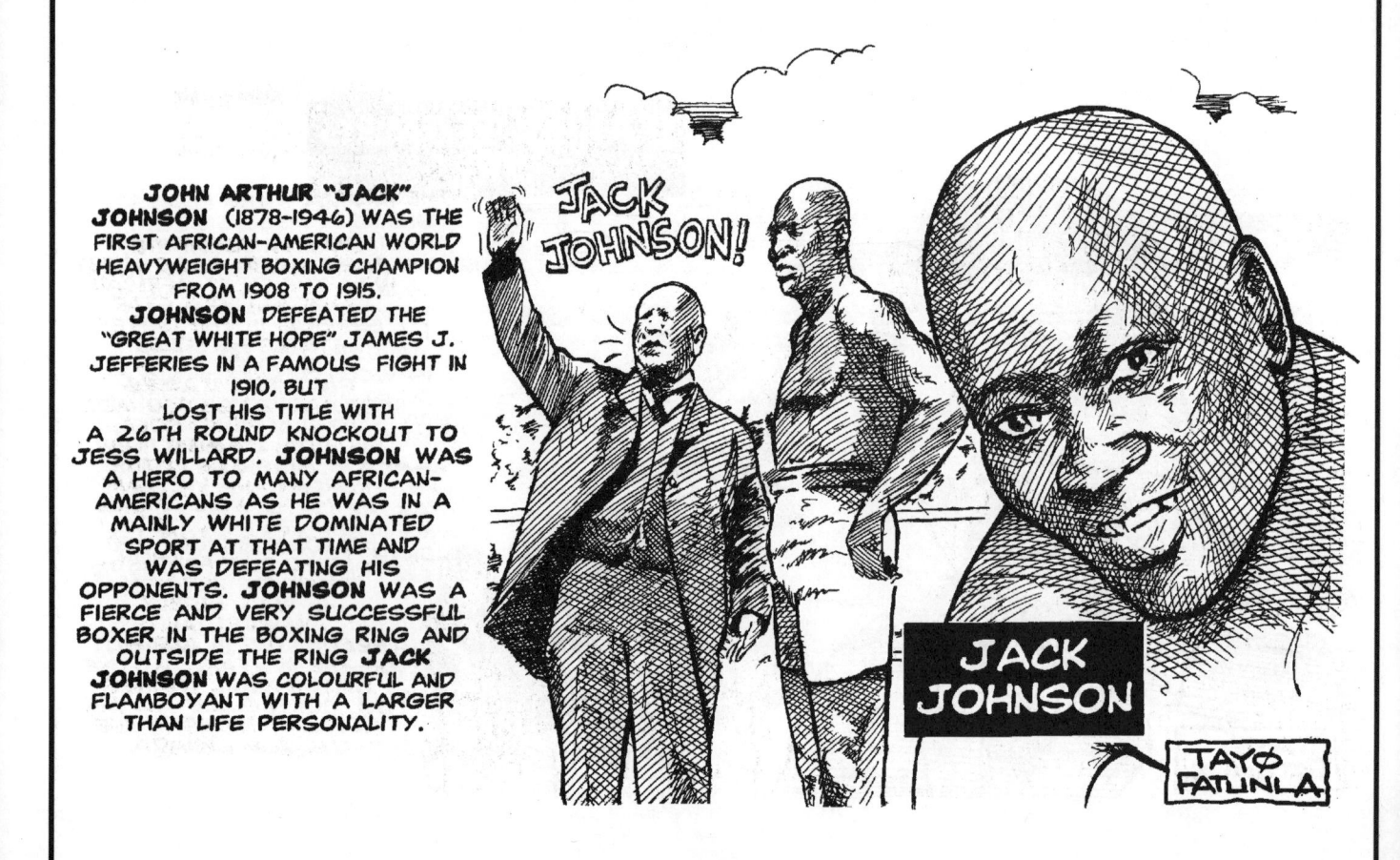

JOHN ARTHUR "JACK" JOHNSON (1878-1946) WAS THE FIRST AFRICAN-AMERICAN WORLD HEAVYWEIGHT BOXING CHAMPION FROM 1908 TO 1915.

JOHNSON DEFEATED THE "GREAT WHITE HOPE" JAMES J. JEFFERIES IN A FAMOUS FIGHT IN 1910, BUT LOST HIS TITLE WITH A 26TH ROUND KNOCKOUT TO JESS WILLARD. JOHNSON WAS A HERO TO MANY AFRICAN-AMERICANS AS HE WAS IN A MAINLY WHITE DOMINATED SPORT AT THAT TIME AND WAS DEFEATING HIS OPPONENTS. JOHNSON WAS A FIERCE AND VERY SUCCESSFUL BOXER IN THE BOXING RING AND OUTSIDE THE RING JACK JOHNSON WAS COLOURFUL AND FLAMBOYANT WITH A LARGER THAN LIFE PERSONALITY.

JACK JOHNSON!

JACK JOHNSON

TAYO FATUNLA

KAABA

THE **KAABA** – THE HOLIEST SHRINE IN MECCA, SAUDI ARABIA, IS A CUBE SHAPED STONE BUILDING COVERED WITH A BLACK CLOTH. IT WAS ADOPTED BY THE PROPHET MOHAMMED (570-632 A.D.) AS A SACRED PLACE OF WORSHIP. IT IS VISITED BY MILLIONS OF MUSLIMS AROUND THE WORLD. MANY AFRICAN AND AFRICAN-AMERICAN MUSLIMS VISIT THE **KAABA** EVERY YEAR. THIS PILGRIMAGE IS CALLED A *HAJ*. THE ISLAMIC RELIGION CAME INTO AFRICA FROM THE NORTH. THIS NEW RELIGION SPREAD INTO NORTH AND EAST AFRICA AND TO SUDAN PARTLY BY CONQUEST AND PARTLY THROUGH TRADE BY THE ARABS. BETWEEN 670 AND 705 A.D. PART OF NORTH AFRICA BECAME AN ESTABLISHED PROVINCE OF THE MUSLIM EMPIRE.

RAJ KAPOOR

RAJ KAPOOR (1924-1988) WAS BORN IN PESHAWAR, INDIA INTO AN ACTING FAMILY. BY THE AGE OF TWENTY THREE, **KAPOOR** WAS THE YOUNGEST PRODUCER AND DIRECTOR IN THE INDIAN FILM INDUSTRY. HE BUILT THE *RAJ KAPOOR* STUDIOS IN 1950. THE FILM AWAARA (THE TRAMP, A ROLE HE ACTED HIMSELF) MADE RK STUDIOS FAMOUS ALL OVER THE WORLD. **KAPOOR** WAS A GREAT ENTERTAINER WHO SINGLE-HANDEDLY MADE THE WHOLE WORLD PAY ATTENTION TO "BOLLYWOOD" MOVIES. HE MADE POPULAR FILMS THAT ALSO FEATURED HIS SONS, RISHI AND RANDHIR. AFTER HIS DEATH *RAJ KAPOOR'S* SONS COMPLETED THE FILM HE DID NOT LIVE TO COMPLETE, TITLED *HENNA*.

TAYO FATUNLA

JONAH LOMU

JONAH LOMU (1975–), USES HIS AWESOME SKILL AND POWER TO HELP MAKE RUGBY EXCITING TO WATCH AND, IN MUCH OF THE WORLD, THE PREFERRED ALTERNATIVE TO AMERICAN FOOTBALL. BORN IN MANGERE, NEW ZEALAND, **LOMU** IS THE YOUNGEST BLACK NEW ZEALANDER IN ANY SPORT TO PLAY FOR HIS COUNTRY'S NATIONAL TEAM. **JONAH LOMU'S** RUGBY DEBUT WAS IN 1994 AGAINST FRANCE.

TAYO FATUNLA

Author, story teller, dramatist and comedienne, **LOUISE BENNETT** (1919 -) was born in Kingston, Jamaica. While in her teens, **MISS LOU**, as she was affectionately known to the public began writing in dialect. Her research and folklore creations for the Jamaican stage helped to save much of Jamaican folk-material from extinction.

MISS LOU was a natural artist. She collected Anancy stories (Anancy is a spider), Jamaican folk-songs, folk-legends, proverbs, riddles and weaved them into her own writings and style. In recognition of **MISS LOU'S** work, she was awarded the MBE by Queen Elizabeth II for work in Jamaican theatre and literature.

Louise Bennett's many recordings include Jamaica Singing Games (1953), **MISS LOU** Views (1967), **MISS LOU** (1981), **MISS LOU** Live in London (1983). **MISS LOU** has been instrumental in promoting Jamaican culture abroad.

ALBERT LUTHULI

Along with the Mandelas, Oliver Tambo and Steve Biko, Chief **Albert Luthuli** (1898-1967) was a leading figure in the liberation of South Africa from the apartheid system. **Luthuli** entered politics in 1945 as a member of the African National Congress (ANC) and rose through the ranks to become president of the party. **Luthuli** had a long-running tense relationship with the apartheid government, which restricted his movements within the country. After the Sharpeville Massacre in 1960, **Luthuli** received the Nobel Peace Prize, becoming the first South African to win the prize. **Albert Luthuli** dedicated his prize to the long-suffering South African people.

TAYO FATUNLA

VAL MCCALLA

The first Black Briton to successfully run a weekly newspaper for Britain's Black community was **VAL MCCALLA** (1943-2002). He arrived in Britain from Jamaica, his "spiritual home", in 1959 and joined the Royal Air Force (RAF) in 1960. There was the need for a voice for the Black British community and with just a loan of five hundred pounds **MCCALLA** published *The Voice* which has a turnover of over five million pounds annually. With a circulation of 54,000 *The Voice* newspaper has sponsored many Black initiatives and has also employed lots of Black Britons who probably would not have had a chance to work in journalism, in many ways, thanks to **VAL MCCALLA'S** vision.

HATTIE MCDANIEL

HATTIE **MCDANIEL** (1895-1952) WAS THE FIRST BLACK ACTOR OR ACTRESS TO WIN AN ACADEMY AWARD. BORN IN WICHITA, KANSAS, **MCDANIEL** PERFORMED ON MANY RADIO AND TELEVISION SHOWS AND USED HER PERSONALITY AND TALENT FOR COMEDY TO MAKE HER SERVANT ROLES IN MOVIES MEMORABLE. SHE MADE HER SERVANT ROLES WISE CHARACTERS. **MCDANIEL'S** ROLE AS "MAMMY" IN THE 1939 CLASSIC *GONE WITH THE WIND* WON HER AN OSCAR FOR BEST SUPPORTING ACTRESS. HATTIE **MCDANIEL** MADE NUMEROUS MOVIES IN THE 1930S AND 1940S.

TAYO FATUNLA

TREVOR MCDONALD

TREVOR MCDONALD (1939-) IS BRITAIN'S FIRST BLACK TELEVISION NEWSCASTER. **MCDONALD** BEGAN HIS CAREER IN TRINIDAD WHERE HE WAS BORN. HE WAS A RADIO PRODUCER FOR THE CARIBBEAN SERVICE IN 1966. HE HAS WORKED FOR BBC RADIO LONDON AND AS A SPORTS CORRESPONDENT WITH INDEPENDENT TELEVISION NEWS (ITN) IN 1973. HE HAS ALSO WORKED ON CHANNEL 4 NEWS, NEWS AT TEN. **MCDONALD** HAS INTERVIEWED MANY WORLD LEADERS INCLUDING SOUTH AFRICA'S PRESIDENT NELSON MANDELA. IN 1992 **TREVOR MCDONALD** WAS AWARDED THE ORDER OF THE BRITISH EMPIRE (OBE) BY THE QUEEN OF ENGLAND.

SAMORA MOISES MACHEL (1933-1986), MOZAMBICAN NATIONALIST AND STATESMAN, WAS LEADER OF THE FRELIMO LIBERATION MOVEMENT (FOUNDED IN 1962) WHICH WON INDEPENDENCE FOR MOZAMBIQUE, AND THUS BECAME ITS FIRST PRESIDENT. AS LEADER, **MACHEL** WAS DYNAMIC. HIS FIRST INITIAL TASK AS PRESIDENT WAS TO SAVE HIS COUNTRY'S ECONOMY AFTER THE MASS EXODUS OF THE PORTUGUESE FARMERS, TECHNICIANS AND MANUFACTURERS FROM MOZAMBIQUE. THIS HE DID WITH SOME SUCCESS. **MACHEL** DEVOTED HIS WHOLE LIFE TO THE STRUGGLE FOR POLITICAL LIBERATION AND TO ESTABLISH SECURITY AND ECONOMIC ORDER IN HIS MOTHERLAND. HE WAS ALSO A THORN IN THE FLESH OF THE APARTHEID GOVERNMENT IN SOUTH AFRICA. **SAMORA MACHEL** DIED IN AN AIR CRASH.

SAMORA MACHEL

TAYO FATUNLA

ADA MCKINLEY

ADA S. **MCKINLEY** (1868-1952) DEVOTED HER LIFE TO AIDING THOSE IN NEED. IN 1919 MCKINLEY FOUNDED "THE SOUTHSIDE SETTLEMENT HOUSE" IN CHICAGO FOR AFRICAN-AMERICANS WHO HAD FOUGHT IN WORLD WAR I AND WANTED A PLACE TO SETTLE AND WORK. MCKINLEY WAS A GREAT WOMAN WHO LEFT A LEGACY OF LOVE AND KINDNESS.

In the nineteenth century in Britain, **Sake Deen Mahomed** (1759-1851) was the most well known professional Asian. He was born in Patna, India and in 1784, he moved to Britain, and settled in Cork, Ireland. Moving to London, **Mahomed** ran a coffee house. Later, he went to Brighton and opened a health establishment in 1815 using herbs and oil. **Mahomed** faced medical opposition and prejudice and his patients stayed away. His success began after he gave free treatment to some patients and they discovered that his remedies worked. People from all walks of life flocked to **Mahomed's** medical baths. King George IV made **Sake Deen Mahomed** his personal "Shampooing Surgeon." He was also known to treat the poor free of charge.

SAKE DEEN MAHOMED

TAYO FATUNLA

NORMAN MANLEY

NORMAN MANLEY (1893-1969), ONE OF THE NATIONAL HEROES OF JAMAICA, WAS A FORMER PREMIER AND CO-FOUNDER OF THE FIRST JAMAICAN MASS BASED POLITICAL PARTY, THE PEOPLE'S NATIONAL PARTY. **MANLEY** BECAME ACTIVE IN JAMAICAN POLITICS IN 1938, AND BY 1959 WHEN JAMAICA ACHIEVED FULL INTERNAL SELF-GOVERNMENT BASED ON A NEW CONSTITUTION, **MANLEY** WAS REGARDED AS THE FATHER OF THE NATIONALIST MOVEMENT. **NORMAN MANLEY** WAS PREMIER OF JAMAICA FROM 1953 TO 1962.

TAYO FATUNLA

THE PROTEST MARCH

TAYO FATUNLA

Another **PROTEST MARCH**, another victorious **MARCH** led by civil rights activist, Dr. Martin Luther King Jr. In the early 1960s. He led crowds of African-Americans to Selma, Dallas County, Alabama. This **MARCH** was King's effort to get everyone to protest about the inequality of voting in the state and to have African-Americans registered to vote. Twenty-eight whites were registered for every African-American registered. It took the intervention of President Johnson to approve a new law providing for direct federal government intervention. This guaranteed registration for the African-Americans who eventually were included in the democratic process.

TRIBAL MARKS

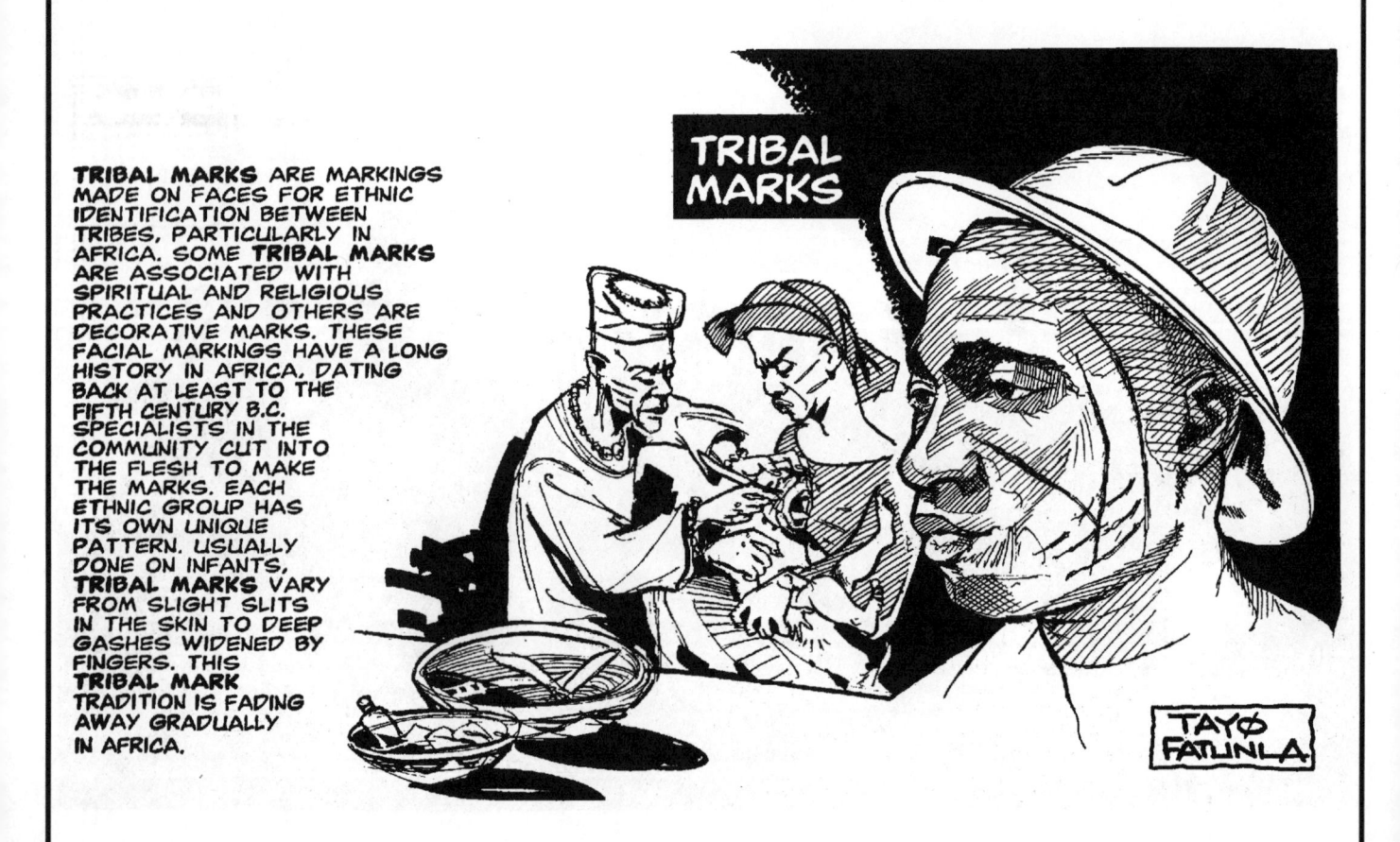

TRIBAL MARKS ARE MARKINGS MADE ON FACES FOR ETHNIC IDENTIFICATION BETWEEN TRIBES, PARTICULARLY IN AFRICA. SOME **TRIBAL MARKS** ARE ASSOCIATED WITH SPIRITUAL AND RELIGIOUS PRACTICES AND OTHERS ARE DECORATIVE MARKS. THESE FACIAL MARKINGS HAVE A LONG HISTORY IN AFRICA, DATING BACK AT LEAST TO THE FIFTH CENTURY B.C. SPECIALISTS IN THE COMMUNITY CUT INTO THE FLESH TO MAKE THE MARKS. EACH ETHNIC GROUP HAS ITS OWN UNIQUE PATTERN. USUALLY DONE ON INFANTS, **TRIBAL MARKS** VARY FROM SLIGHT SLITS IN THE SKIN TO DEEP GASHES WIDENED BY FINGERS. THIS **TRIBAL MARK** TRADITION IS FADING AWAY GRADUALLY IN AFRICA.

TAYO FATUNLA

THURGOOD MARSHALL (1908-1993) WAS THE FIRST AFRICAN-AMERICAN TO BE APPOINTED TO THE UNITED STATES SUPREME COURT (1967-1991). **MARSHALL** WAS MORE THAN A LAWYER, HE WAS A CRUSADER FOR COMMON JUSTICE. **MARSHALL** MORE THAN ANY ONE ELSE MADE AN IMPACT IN THE LONG STRUGGLE FOR CIVIL RIGHTS IN THE U.S. BORN IN BALTIMORE, MARYLAND, **MARSHALL** STUDIED LAW AT HOWARD UNIVERSITY. HE BECAME A COUNSEL FOR THE NAACP, THEN A CHIEF COUNSEL BEFORE PRESIDENT JOHN F. KENNEDY NAMED HIM TO THE U.S. COURT OF APPEAL. THE SON OF A SLEEPING CAR PORTER, **MARSHALL** WAS ELEVATED TO THE U.S. SUPREME COURT BY PRESIDENT JOHNSON. AN IMPORTANT CASE THAT WAS ASSOCIATED WITH **THURGOOD MARSHALL** WAS THE CASE OF BROWN V. BROWN (1954) WHICH OVERTURNED PLESSY V. FERGUSON (1896) AND MADE ILLEGAL THE "SEPARATE BUT EQUAL" POLICY THAT INFACT PERPETUATED SEGREGATION AND INFERIOR EDUCATION FOR AFRICAN-AMERICANS.

THURGOOD MARSHALL

TAYO FATUNLA

NANNY THE MAROON IS CONSIDERED TO HAVE LED THE **MAROONS** OF JAMAICA TO RAID AND AMBUSH BRITISH SOLDIERS SENT IN THE 17TH CENTURY ONWARDS TO ENFORCE SLAVERY AND PUT DOWN THE INSURRECTION. BRITAIN IN THE END, WAS FORCED TO SIGN A TREATY WHICH GAVE THE **MAROONS** A FREE STATE WITHIN THE COLONY. **MAROONS** WERE AFRICANS WHO RESISTED ENSLAVEMENT BY LIVING IN THE MOUNTAINS AND FORESTS OF JAMAICA. "QUEEN OF THE MOUNTAIN" **NANNY** PLAYED A KEY ROLE IN THE FOUNDING OF **MAROON** NATION.

AN OBEAH (TRADITIONAL OCCULTIST) WOMAN, SHE USED HER RITUAL POWERS TO ALSO FIGHT THE ENEMY. **NANNY'S** ROLE IN WAR IS A SYMBOL OF RESISTANCE TO BLACK WOMEN AND IN PARTICULAR TO JAMAICAN WOMEN. **NANNY THE MAROON'S** IMAGE GRACES THE JAMAICAN $500 BILL.

NANNY THE MAROON

TAYO FATUNLA

MASOPHA

MASOPHA (1820-1899) WAS THE THIRD SON OF KING MOSHOESHOE. MOSHOESHOE FOUNDED THE SOTHO NATION, NOW CALLED LESOTHO IN SOUTHERN AFRICA. **MASOPHA** LED HIS COUNTRY IN A SUCCESSFUL REVOLT AGAINST THE CAPE ADMINISTRATION IN SOUTH AFRICA UNDER THE BRITISH RULE. **MASOPHA** CONTINUED HIS FIGHT FOR INDEPENDENCE. HE WAS AGGRESSIVE AND TROUBLESOME BUT HE WAS INSTRUMENTAL IN LESOTHO EVENTUALLY BECOMING AN INDEPENDENT NATION IN 1966.

TAYO FATUNLA

THE MAYAS

Originally from around 2500 B.C., **THE MAYAS** occupied a wide region in areas now included in states such as Mexico, Guatemala, Elsalvador, the western part of Honduras and Belise in Central America. **THE MAYAS** of today still live in villages where their ancestors created their high and rich culture. **THE MAYA** architecture was based on religious beliefs and this is why temples and palaces were built in the centre of the cities while ordinary homes were on the outskirts. The most outstanding building at Chichen Itza is the Castillo, built by **THE MAYAS. THE MAYAS** of today combine pre-hispanic and Roman Catholic beliefs. They worship the gods of nature and perform rituals to control weather and for curing sickness which are directed by specialists in the supernatural.

JOHN MITCHELL JR.

JOHN MITCHELL JR. (1863-1929) WAS A CRUSADING AFRICAN-AMERICAN JOURNALIST WHO SPOKE AND WROTE THE TRUTH WITHOUT FEAR IN HIS TIME. **MITCHELL JR.** WAS BORN IN RICHMOND, VIRGINIA. HE PURSUED A TEACHING CAREER FOR A WHILE AND IN 1884 TOOK CONTROL OF THE WEEKLY NEWSPAPER, *THE RICHMOND PLANET*. THE PAPER WAS WELL KNOWN FOR ITS INVESTIGATIVE JOURNALISM INTO LYNCHINGS AND THE MURDERS OF AFRICAN-AMERICANS WHICH OCCURED IN THE SOUTH. **JOHN MITCHELL JR.** EARNED THE REPUTATION OF A VIGOROUS AND MILITANT EDITOR AND HE CONTINUED TO RALLY AGAINST RACIAL INJUSTICES UP TILL THE TIME OF HIS DEATH.

After nearly 32 years in power, **MOBUTU SESE SEKO** (1930-1997) was overthrown as the head of state of Zaire in Central Africa renamed the Democratic Republic of Congo after his fall. **MOBUTU** came to symbolise self-enrichment and extravagance in excess. **MOBUTU** seized power in 1965 which was welcomed by the West. He cemented his dictatorship by ensuring that his powerful opponents ceased to be a threat to him. **MOBUTU** had a policy of "Zairanization" to shake off remnants of colonial rule. Originally named Joseph Desire **MOBUTU**, he began by changing his name and he also changed his country's name from Congo to Zaire in 1971 after renaming major cities. **MOBUTU** played an important role in African affairs particularly in Angola, Chad, Rwanda, Burundi and the Central African Republic. **MOBUTU SESE SEKO** died in exile in Morocco.

MOBUTU SESE SEKO

TAYO FATUNLA

RONALD MOODY

One of Britain's outstanding post Second World War black sculptors was **Ronald Moody** (1900-1984). **Moody** was born in Jamaica and moved to England in 1923 to study dentistry. An admirer of Egyptian artefacts, **Moody** turned to sculpture. He exhibited his bronze and carvings in France in 1937. In 1940, Germany invaded France and **Moody** moved back to England where he became a regular exhibitor at the Royal Academy. One of his biggest commissioned pieces was for the Jamaica Government. **Moody** produced a sculpture of *the Savcou bird of Carib Mythology* (1963). **Ronald Moody** was awarded Jamaica's Musgrave Gold Medal (1978) for contributions to culture and the Minority Rights Award for contributions to sculpture in Britain.

ASKIA MUHAMMAD (1493-1528) REIGNED AS KING OF THE SONGHAY EMPIRE IN WEST AFRICA FOR THIRTY-FIVE YEARS. **ASKIA** RULED IN ACCORDANCE WITH ISLAMIC TEACHINGS AND TRADITIONS. AS A SUCCESSFUL MILITARY COMMANDER, HE IS KNOWN TO HAVE DEVELOPED A STRONG CENTRALIZED GOVERNMENT IN HIS EMPIRE. UNDER HIS LEADERSHIP, SONGHAY BECAME THE LARGEST AND THE MOST POWERFUL OF THE WEST AFRICAN EMPIRES. **ASKIA MUHAMMAD** WAS RESPONSIBLE FOR A SERIES OF "JIHADS" (HOLY WARS).

ASKIA MUHAMMAD

TAYO FATUNLA

ELIJAH MUHAMMED

ELIJAH MUHAMMED (1897-1975) JOINED THE NATION OF ISLAM, AN AFRICAN-AMERICAN ORGANISATION ALSO CALLED "BLACK MUSLIMS" AT ABOUT 1930. **MUHAMMED** WAS BORN ELIJAH POOLE IN GEORGIA. IN 1934 AFTER THE DISAPPEARANCE OF POOLE'S SPIRITUAL LEADER, THE NATION OF ISLAM'S FOUNDER WALI FARAD, POOLE EMERGED AS **ELIJAH MUHAMMED** THE DIVINE LEADER. UNDER HIS LEADERSHIP, SEPARATE SCHOOLS, FARMS AND SMALL BUSINESSES WERE CREATED TO BE RUN BY AND FOR BLACK PEOPLE. **MUHAMMED** INSTILLED A SENSE OF POWER AND PERSONAL WORTH IN BLACK PEOPLE. AFTER HIS DEATH, **ELIJAH MUHAMMED'S** SON WALLACE TOOK OVER HIS LEADERSHIP.

TAYO FATUNLA

HUEY NEWTON

"THE BLACK PANTHER IS AN ANIMAL THAT WHEN IT IS PRESSURED, IT MOVES BACK UNTIL IT IS CORNERED, THEN COMES OUT FIGHTING FOR LIFE OR DEATH". **HUEY P. NEWTON** (1942-1989) WAS CO-FOUNDER OF THE BLACK PANTHER PARTY IN THE U.S. WITH BOBBY SEALE. IT BEGAN IN OAKLAND, CALIFORNIA IN 1966 FOR THE SELF-DEFENCE. THE PARTY INITIALLY FORMED TO MONITOR THE ACTIVITIES OF POLICE WHO PATROLLED OAKLAND'S BLACK COMMUNITY. LATER ON, IT BEGAN TO ADDRESS THE SOCIAL, ECONOMIC AND POLITICAL IMBALANCE AND AS SUCH BROADEN ITS VIEWS. **NEWTON** WAS MINISTER OF DEFENCE OF THE PARTY. HE WAS CHARGED WITH THE MANSLAUGHTER OF A POLICE OFFICER BUT HIS CONVICTION WAS OVERTURNED.
LOVE HIM OR HATE HIM, **HUEY P. NEWTON** WAS A HERO TO THOUSANDS OF PEOPLE.

LILIAN NGOYI

THE FIRST WOMAN EVER TO BE ELECTED TO THE NATIONAL EXECUTIVE COMMITTEE OF SOUTH AFRICA'S AFRICAN NATIONAL CONGRESS WAS **LILIAN NGOYI** (1911-1980).

SHE WAS THE MOST TALKED ABOUT WOMAN IN SOUTH AFRICA'S POLITICS IN THE FIFTIES. ENERGETIC **NGOYI** WAS BORN IN PRETORIA AND SHE PLAYED AN IMPORTANT PART IN THE LIBERATION STRUGGLE IN SOUTH AFRICA. BANNING ORDERS FROM THE THEN APARTHEID GOVERNMENT PROHIBITING HER FROM ATTENDING MEETINGS DID NOT STOP HER FROM SPEAKING OUT. **MA-NGOYI**, AS SHE WAS AFFECTIONATELY KNOWN BY HER COMRADES, FOUGHT FOR WOMEN'S HUMAN RIGHTS, AND STRUGGLED FOR A BETTER LIFE FOR ALL HUMANITY.

TAYO FATUNLA

JOSHUA NKOMO

JOSHUA NKOMO OF THE NDEBELE PEOPLE WAS BORN IN 1917 AT SEMOKWE, SOUTHERN RHODESIA, THE PRESENT ZIMBABWE. HE WAS ONE OF THE FOUNDING FATHERS OF ZIMBABWE AND A PAN-AFRICANIST. IN 1948 **NKOMO** BECAME THE PRESIDENT OF SOUTHERN RHODESIA'S AFRICAN NATIONAL CONGRESS. HE CAMPAIGNED FOR DEMOCRATIC GOVERNMENT IN HIS COUNTRY. HE WAS PRESIDENT OF ZAPU, THE ZIMBABWE AFRICAN PEOPLES' UNION, IN 1962 AS HIS PARTY EVOLVED **NKOMO** WAS IMPRISONED FOR HIS CAMPAIGNING, BETWEEN 1964 AND 1974. IN 1983 HE ESCAPED WHAT HE SAID WAS A MURDER PLOT BY GOVERNMENT FORCES IN THE NEWLY INDEPENDENT ZIMBABWE AND FLED TO BRITAIN. **NKOMO** RETURNED LATER TO ZIMBABWE TO CONTINUE IN ACTIVE POLITICS AND HE WAS THE VICE-PRESIDENT FROM 1990. **JOHSUA NKOMO**, A GIANT BOTH PHYSICALLY AND POLITICALLY, DIED IN 1999.

TAYO FATUNLA

NICHELLE NICHOLS, A SINGER, EDUCATOR, DANCER AND ACTRESS, WAS THE FIRST AFRICAN-AMERICAN WOMAN TO HAVE A MAJOR CONTINUING ROLE ON AMERICAN TELEVISION. OVERCOMING RACISM, **NICHOLS** DEVELOPED INTO AN ACCOMPLISHED ACTRESS. BY THE AGE OF SIXTEEN SHE HAD WORKED WITH DUKE ELLINGTON. **NICHOLS** MET GENE RODENBURY, CREATOR OF THE SUCCESSFUL SCIENCE FICTION SERIES, "STAR TREK." SHE PLAYED LIEUTENANT UHURA, A COMMUNICATIONS OFFICER OF THE STAR SHIP *ENTERPRISE*. **NICHELLE NICHOLS'** BIGGEST ROLE, HOWEVER, WAS AS AN ENTERTAINMENT PIONEER.

NICHELLE NICHOLS

TAYO FATUNLA

JULIUS NYERERE, OF TANZANIA IN EAST AFRICA, WAS BORN IN 1922. **NYERERE** BEGAN HIS POLITICAL LIFE BY JOINING THE TANGANYIKA AFRICAN ASSOCIATION, FORMED TO PROVIDE A DISCUSSION FORUM FOR AFRICAN OPINION; LATER HE LED THE TANZANIA AFRICAN NATIONAL UNION (TANU). IN 1960, HE BECAME THE PRIME MINISTER OF TANGANYIKA AND FOUR YEARS LATER HE BECAME THE FIRST PRESIDENT OF A UNITED TANZANIA. **NYERERE** WAS KNOWN AS THE MOST ORIGINAL THINKER OF AFRICA'S POLITICAL PERSONALITIES. IN 1985 HE STOOD DOWN FROM THE PRESIDENCY BUT DID NOT RETIRE FROM POLITCS. **JULIUS NYERERE** WHO WAS CALLED "MWALIMU" (TEACHER), DIED IN 1999.

MWALIMU

TAYO FATUNLA

JULIUS NYERERE

HENRY NXUMALO

THE LATE GREAT **HENRY NXUMALO** (1917-1957) WAS A SOUTH AFRICAN SPORTS WRITER, JOURNALIST AND AUTHOR IN THE APARTHEID YEARS. IN 1951 **NXUMALO** BECAME A SPORTS EDITOR OF *THE DRUM* WHERE HE CREATED STUNTS TO RAISE THE PROFILE OF THE MAGAZINE. **NXUMALO** WAS WELL KNOWN FOR HIS INVESTIGATIVE JOURNALISM EXPOSING CRUELTY, INJUSTICE AND NARROW-MINDEDNESS, WHICH DID NOT GO DOWN WELL IN SOME QUARTERS. HE INVESTIGATED A WHITE SOUTH AFRICAN DOCTOR WHO HAD PERFORMED ILLEGAL ABORTIONS IN THE WESTERN NATIVE TOWNSHIPS AND WHOSE KNIFE SEVERAL WOMEN HAD DIED FROM. **HENRY NXUMALO** DIED A VICTIM OF THE WHITE-DOMINATED SOUTH AFRICA'S VIOLENCE.

TAYO FATUNLA

GEORGE PEMBA

GEORGE MILWA PEMBA (1911-2001) WAS AN EARLY PIONEER ARTIST OF SOUTH AFRICA. THROUGHOUT HIS LIFE, **PEMBA** LIVED FOR ART. **PEMBA** WAS BORN AT KORSTEN IN THE CAPE PROVINCE. HIS DRAWINGS VARIED FROM PORTRAITURE TO LANDSCAPES, TOWNSHIPS AND MARKET SCENES AND ETCHING FOR A NUMBER OF AFRICAN CHIEFS AND PROMINENT PERSONALITIES. AMONG HIS BEST KNOWN DRAWINGS WAS ONE OF CHIEF A.J. LUTHULI PRESIDENT OF THE ANC IN THE FIFTIES. **GEORGE PEMBA** HELD SERIES OF ONE MAN SHOWS AT PORT ELIZABETH AND EAST LONDON AND ALSO CONTRIBUTED TO ANNUAL EXHIBITIONS. HE WAS AN ILLUSTRATOR OF MANY BOOKS AND HE IS AMONG THE GREAT ARTISTS AFRICA HAS PRODUCED.

KING PIANKHI

KING PIANKHI (753-713 B.C.) WAS A KUSHITE (FROM KUSH IN WHAT IS NOW SUDAN) WHO UNITED NUBIA, MEROE, KUSH AND EGYPT UNDER ONE EMPIRE. AFRICAN RULERS DREAMED OF RECAPTURING UPPER EGYPT FROM THE RULE OF INVADERS FROM ASIA, BUT THE DREAM SEEMED IMPOSSIBLE UNTIL **KING PIANKHI** TURNED DREAM INTO REALITY DURING HIS REIGN. **PIANKHI** WAS THE THIRD RULER OF THE TWENTY-FIFTH DYNASTY OF EGYPT.

TAYO FATUNLA

MARTIN PORRES

SAINT MARTIN DE PORRES (1579-1639) WAS THE FIRST BLACK TO BE CANONIZED IN THE CATHOLIC CHURCH IN MODERN TIMES. HE WAS BORN IN PERU, SOUTH AMERICA, AS THE SON OF A SPANISH KNIGHT AND ANNA, A BLACK FREED WOMAN FROM PANAMA. IN 1954, **SAINT MARTIN DE PORRES** BECAME A DOMINICAN LAY BROTHER AND WON AN EXCEPTIONAL REPUTATION FOR HIS WORK WITH THE SICK AND POOR AND FOR HIS HOLINESS.

TAYO FATUNLA

"MR. CIVIL RIGHTS", **ADAM CLAYTON POWELL, JR.** (1908-1972) WAS A FLAMBOYANT UNITED STATES CONGRESSMAN WHO FOUGHT AGAINST LARGE CORPORATIONS TO MAKE THEM DROP THEIR UNOFFICIAL BANS ON EMPLOYING AFRICAN-AMERICANS. HE HELPED TO ORGANIZE A RELIEF OPERATION FOR THE THOUSANDS OF HARLEM'S NEEDY HABITANTS IN NEW YORK. WHEREVER **POWELL, JR.** WENT, HE DREW ATTENTION TO DISCRIMINATORY PRACTICES HE COULD NOT OVERLOOK, INCLUDING ON THE CAPITOL HILL. **POWELL, JR.** DEMANDED THAT AN AFRICAN-AMERICAN JOURNALIST BE ALLOWED TO SIT IN THE SENATE AND HOUSE OF REPRESENTATIVES PRESS GALLERIES. **POWELL, JR.** WAS BORN RAISED IN NEW YORK. HE WAS ELECTED TO CONGRESS IN 1944. **ADAM CLAYTON POWELL, JR.** RETIRED FROM POLITICS IN 1970.

ADAM CLAYTON POWELL, JR.

TAYO FATUNLA

PREMPEH II

OTUMFUO OSEI AGYEMAN PREMPEH II, ASANTEHENE (1892-1970) WAS A DESCENDANT OF OSEI TUTU, FOUNDER OF THE ASHANTI EMPIRE IN GHANA. PREMPEH II WAS THE SPIRITUAL HEAD OF THE ASHANTI RELIGION. AS AN OCCUPIER OF THE GOLDEN STOOL. PREMPEH II WAS A KING OF AUTHORITY AND WAS WELL ADMIRED. THE GOLDEN STOOL IS BELIEVED BY MANY ASHANTIS TO HAVE BEEN CALLED FROM THE SKY IN THE SEVENTEENTH CENTURY. EACH LEG OF THE GOLDEN STOOL INCORPORATES A KNOT OF WISDOM.

ROLAND RAMPAT

ROLAND RAMPAT (1948-) WAS BORN IN THE FORMER BRITISH GUIANA, NOW KNOWN AS GUYANA, IN SOUTH AMERICA OF INDENTURED INDIAN AND WELSH ANCESTRY. **RAMPAT** EMIGRATED TO THE UNITED KINGDOM AT THE AGE OF 21. DETERMINED TO MAKE IT, **RAMPAT** STUDIED ACCOUNTANCY AT A NIGHT SCHOOL AND WORKED DURING THE DAY TO MAKE ENDS MEET. 1976 WAS A TURNING POINT FOR **RAMPAT** WHEN HE JOINED EUROPA WORLDWIDE LOGISTICS (A FREIGHT DELIVERY COMPANY) AS THE COMPANY'S ACCOUNTANT. **RAMPAT** WENT ON TO BECOME EUROPA'S COMPANY SECRETARY AND EVENTUALLY, ITS DIRECTOR. **ROLAND RAMPAT** HAS EMBRACED THE CULTURAL AWARENESS OF BLACK HISTORY WITH ALL HIS HEART. HE HAS RAISED OVER 500,000 POUNDS FOR CHARITIES SUCH AS RED CROSS AND THE GREAT ORMOND STREET HOSPITAL IN LONDON.

ASA RANDOLPH

ASA PHILLIP RANDOLPH (1889-1979) WAS A GREAT TRADE UNION ORGANIZER. HE SPENT FORTY YEARS OF HIS LIFE TO ENSURE BETTER WORKING CONDITIONS AND HIGHER WAGES FOR ALL LABOURERS. BORN IN FLORIDA, RANDOLPH WAS THE FOUNDER OF THE BROTHERHOOD OF SLEEPING CAR PORTERS IN 1937. THIS AFRICAN-AMERICAN UNION SIGNED ITS FIRST CONTRACT EVER WITH AN AMERICAN CORPORATION, AND SO HISTORY WAS MADE.

They may have wild looks and live by a philosophy of peace and brothely love. **RASTAFARIANS**, RASTAS as they are called, grow their hair without combing until it twists and mats into locks called dreadlocks. Some dreadlocks may dangle below the waist. **RASTAFARIANS** are guided by a biblical passage in the Old Testament, Leviticus 21:5. Their prophet is Marcus Garvey (1887-1940), Jamaica's national hero. Emperor Haile Selassie is seen by them to be the direct descendant of King Solomon, and therefore they adopted Haile Selassie's early name (Rastafari) for themselves. They also see themselves as one of the lost tribes of Israel who were exiled into Babylon. **RASTAFARIANS** are non-smokers but smoking ganja (marijuana), called "Wisdom Weed" or "Sacred Herb", is seen as a religious act accompanied with prayers and the reading of Psalms. **RASTAFARIANS** take great pride in black heritage. Among the well known Rastas who put Jamaica on the world map was Bob Marley. His song reflected the beliefs of **RASTAFARIANS**. Women **RASTAFARIANS** keep their hair covered.

RASTAFARIANS

TAYO FATUNLA

SUGAR RAY ROBINSON

SUGAR RAY ROBINSON MADE HISTORY BY BEING THE FIRST AFRICAN-AMERICAN TO WIN A WORLD BOXING TITLE FIVE TIMES. **ROBINSON** GREW UP IN DETROIT WATCHING HIS IDOL JOE LOUIS TRAIN TO FIGHT. AS AN AMATEUR, HE TRAINED IN HARLEM, NEW YORK. WHEN IT WAS TIME FOR ROBINSON TO FIGHT IN THE RING, HE WON THE MIDDLE-WEIGHT TITLE ON FEBRUARY 14, 1951, SEPTEMBER 12, 1951, DECEMBER 9, 1955, MAY 1, 1957 AND MARCH 25, 1958. **ROBINSON** ALSO TOOK THE WELTER-WEIGHT TITLE FROM JAKE LAMOTA. HIS PUNCHES WERE DEVASTATING. **SUGAR RAY ROBINSON** (REAL NAME WALTER SMITH) DIED IN 1989. HIS LAST FIGHT WAS AT THE AGE OF 45.

TAYO FATUNLA

WALTER RODNEY

WALTER RODNEY (1942-1980) WAS A LECTURER IN AFRICAN HISTORY AT DAR-ES-SALAAM UNIVERSITY, TANZANIA FOR SEVEN YEARS. A NATIVE OF GUYANA, HE RETURNED HOME IN 1974 AND BECAME A MEMBER OF THE OPPOSITION WORKING PEOPLE'S ALLIANCE. HIS ACADEMIC PAPERS AND ARTICLES WERE PUBLISHED IN MAGAZINES AND JOURNALS WORLDWIDE. HIS MOST NOTABLE WORKS INCLUDE *HOW EUROPE UNDERDEVELOPED AFRICA* (1972) AND *A HISTORY OF THE WORKING PEOPLE OF GUYANA* (1981).

J.A. ROGERS

SELF-TRAINED **JOEL AUGUSTUS ROGERS** (1880-1966) IN HIS LIFETIME, REVEALED NUMEROUS FACTS ABOUT THE BLACK RACE. **ROGERS** WAS A WORLD TRAVELLER AND AN ACCOMPLISHED LECTURER. HE MADE HISTORY BY BECOMING THE FIRST BLACK WAR CORRESPONDENT FOR THE NEW YORK AMSTERDAM NEWS. **ROGERS** WAS BORN IN JAMAICA. HE MOVED TO THE UNITED STATES AND SETTLED IN NEW YORK. BETWEEN 1925 AND 1936, **ROGERS** TRAVELLED TO EUROPE AND AFRICA INVESTIGATING IN LIBRARIES AND MUSEUMS, THE HISTORY OF AFRICAN PEOPLE. NO PUBLISHING HOUSE WOULD PUBLISH HIS WORKS AND FINDINGS SO **JOEL ROGERS** WENT INTO SELF-PUBLISHING THEREBY PUBLISHING MANY OF HIS WORKS HIMSELF. HIS TEXT COVERED GLOBAL AFRICA, ASIA, AUSTRALIA, SOUTH PACIFIC, EUROPE AND WESTERN HEMISPHERE. ONE OF HIS FINDINGS, WAS THAT THE SWASTIKA, EMBLEM OF NAZI GERMANY WAS USED BY THE BLACK PEOPLE OF EASTER ISLAND, POLYNESIA AND ELAM IN SOUTHERN PERSIA MORE THAN 7000 YEARS BEFORE.

KEN SARO-WIWA

KEN SARO-WIWA (1941-1995) WAS A NIGERIAN WRITER, POLITICAL ACTIVIST AND ENVIRONMENTAL CAMPAIGNER.

SARO-WIWA WAS WELL KNOWN FOR THE MANY BOOKS HE WROTE. HE BECAME INTERNATIONALLY FAMOUS FOR CHAMPIONING THE CAUSE OF HIS OWN PEOPLE, THE OGONIS OF THE NIGER DELTA IN NIGERIA, IN THEIR THEIR QUEST FOR AN EQUITABLE SHARE OF THE OIL REVENUE EMANATING FROM THEIR LAND. **SARO-WIWA**, TOGETHER WITH MEMBERS OF HIS ETHNIC GROUP, FORMED THE MOVEMENT FOR THE SURVIVAL OF THE OGONI PEOPLE (MOSOP). **SARO-WIWA** WAS EXECUTED IN 1995 WITH EIGHT OTHERS. THE GOVERNMENT THEN ALLEGED THAT THEY WERE RESPONSIBLE FOR THE MURDERS OF FOUR PROMINENT OGONI LEADERS. **KEN SARO-WIWA'S** PRISON NOTES ABOUT HIS DETENTION WERE PUBLISHED POSTHUMOUSLY.

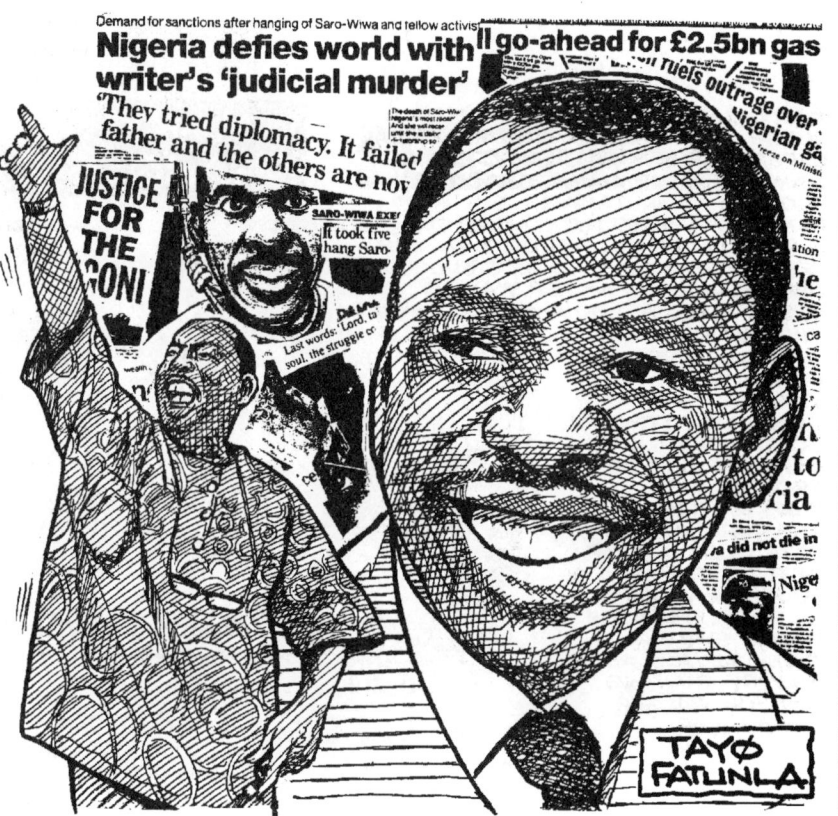

MARY SEACOLE

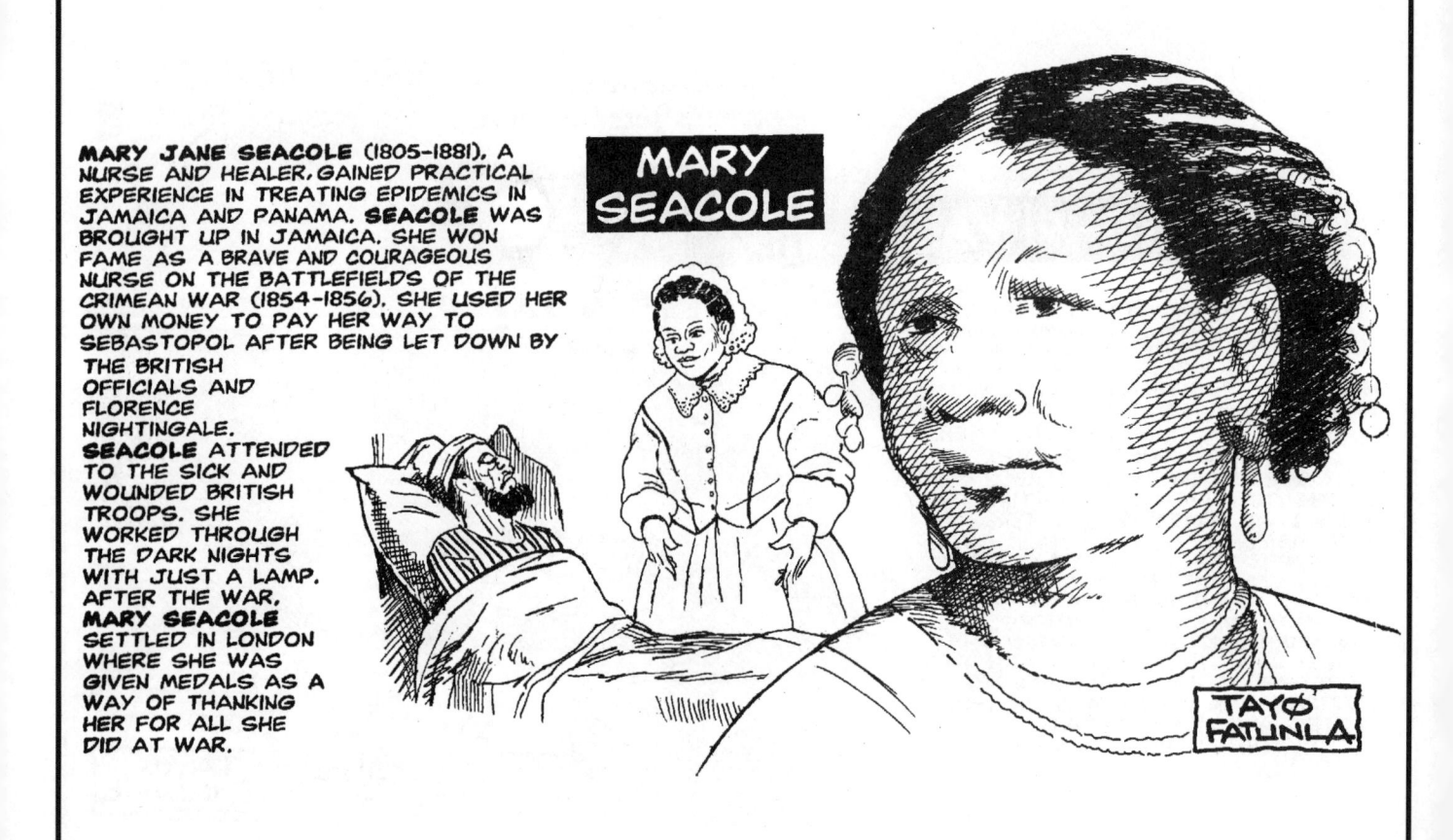

MARY JANE SEACOLE (1805-1881), a nurse and healer, gained practical experience in treating epidemics in Jamaica and Panama. **SEACOLE** was brought up in Jamaica. She won fame as a brave and courageous nurse on the battlefields of the Crimean War (1854-1856). She used her own money to pay her way to Sebastopol after being let down by the British officials and Florence Nightingale. **SEACOLE** attended to the sick and wounded British troops. She worked through the dark nights with just a lamp. After the war, **MARY SEACOLE** settled in London where she was given medals as a way of thanking her for all she did at war.

TAYO FATUNLA

LEOPOLD SENGHOR

UPON INDEPENDENCE IN 1960, RENOWNED AUTHOR, POET AND SENEGALESE STATESMAN **LEOPOLD SENGHOR** (1906-2001) BECAME THE FIRST PRESIDENT OF SENEGAL, A NATION IN WEST AFRICA (WHICH HAS BEEN ONE OF THE FREER COUNTRIES IN AFRICA). **SENGHOR** FAVOURED CLOSE TIES BETWEEN SENEGAL AND FRANCE. HIS PARTY THE BLOC *DEMOCRATIQUE SENEGALAISE* (BDS) LATER REPLACED BY THE *PROGRESSISTE SENEGALAISE* (UPS) IN 1958, DOMINATED SENEGALESE POLITICAL LIFE FOR YEARS FROM 1951, IN 1976 **SENGHOR** INTRODUCED A MULTI-PARTY SYSTEM IN SENEGAL LONG BEFORE MOST OTHER AFRICAN STATES DID SO. SENGHOR WAS RECOGNISED AS ONE OF THE LEADING STATESMEN OF FRENCH-SPEAKING AFRICA. IN 1980 **LEOPOLD SENGHOR** WAS THE FIRST ELECTED AFRICAN HEAD OF STATE TO RETIRE VOLUNTARILY. HE WAS ALSO A LITERARY GIANT; **SENGHOR'S** FIRST ANTHOLOGY OF POEMS WAS PUBLISHED IN 1945 (*CHANTS D'OMBRE*).

TAYO FATUNLA

TUPAC SHAKUR

Controversial as he may have been, **TUPAC AMARU SHAKUR** (1971-1996) is easily the most recognizable icon to emerge from African-American rap/hiphop music. **TUPAC**, or **2PAC** as he was and still is called today had his breakthrough in his chosen career with the release of his first rap album, *2PACALYPSE NOW*. His first crossover hit was in 1993 with the hit song *I GET AROUND*. **TUPAC** had power in his music and he was an embodiment of the music of African-American youth. He ventured into film making and starred in movies such as *POETIC JUSTICE*, *ABOVE THE RUN* and *BULLET* and *GRIDLOCKED*. **TUPAC SHAKUR** was only twenty-five years when he was shot in Las Vegas.

SLAVERY

BELIEVE IT OR NOT, BETWEEN THE 15TH AND 19TH CENTURIES, IT WAS ALWAYS AFRICANS WHO CAPTURED SLAVES, TOOK THEM TO THE COAST AND SOLD THEM TO EUROPEAN TRADERS. MOST AFRICAN KINGDOMS SUCH AS THE BENIN KINGDOM PRACTICED SLAVERY LONG BEFORE EUROPEANS CAME TO THE AFRICAN SHORES. SLAVES WERE CAPTURED IN RAIDS, OR WAR OR WERE FORCED INTO SLAVERY THROUGH POVERTY. SLAVES WERE SOLD TO THE EUROPEAN TRADERS IN RETURN FOR TEXTILES, BOOZE, IRON BARS AND BEADS. WHEN THE EUROPEAN BUYERS OFFERED TOO LITTLE, THE AFRICAN TRADERS REFUSED TO SELL THEIR SLAVES AND THE SLAVE CAPTAINS WOULD SIT OFFSHORE WITH THEIR GOODS TILL THEY COULD SIT NO MORE AND CAVED IN TO THE DEMANDS BY RAISING THEIR OFFERS. THE PORTUGUESE WERE THE MAJOR SLAVE EXPORTERS AT FIRST, THE BRITISH LATER.

TAYO FATUNLA

DAMILOLA TAYLOR

"I WANT TO BE THE VERY BEST LIKE NO ONE EVER HAS BEEN". THE WORDS OF **DAMILOLA TAYLOR** (1989-2000) WHO LIVED A SHORT LIFE ON EARTH. HIS TRAGIC KILLING AT THE HANDS OF UNKNOWN GANG OF YOUTHS IN PECKHAM, IN SOUTH EAST LONDON TOUCHED MANY PEOPLE, NOT JUST IN THE COMMUNITY WHERE HE LIVED BUT IN THE WIDER COMMUNITY OF THE WORLD. PRIME MINISTER TONY BLAIR REMARKED THAT *"SOMETHING GOOD MUST COME OUT OF THE TRAGEDY"*. **TAYLOR** WAS BORN IN NIGERIA AND MOVED TO SOUTH LONDON WITH HIS FAMILY. HIS DEATH AWAKENED THE AUTHORITIES AND FORCED THE LAW TO FACE HARSH REALITIES AND MADE PARENTS, COMMUNITIES AND OFFICIALS MORE AWARE THAN EVER OF THEIR RESPONSIBILITIES TOWARDS YOUNG PEOPLE. **DAMILOLA TAYLOR'S** DEATH WAS NOT IN VAIN.

DAMILOLA TAYLOR R.I.P

TAYO FATUNLA

DALEY THOMPSON

DALEY THOMPSON (1958-) IS BRITAIN'S BEST DECATHLON ATHLETE AND PROBABLY THE WORLD'S GREATEST DECATHLON CHAMPION. **THOMPSON** WAS AN ALL-ROUND ATHLETE IN THE 1980S, WHO RAN, THREW AND JUMPED IN THE TEN EVENT ULTIMATE TEST. HE COMPETED IN HIS FIRST DECATHLON IN 1975 AND WON 19 DECATHLONS IN ALL.

DALEY THOMPSON IS THE FIRST ATHLETE EVER TO HOLD THE COMMONWEALTH, EUROPEAN AND OLYMPIC TITLES AT THE SAME TIME.

TAYO FATUNLA

TIPPU TIB

TIPPU-TIB (1837-1905), A POWERFUL AFRICAN TRADER AND RULER WHO HELPED EUROPEAN EXPLORERS, WAS BORN IN ZANZIBAR AS HAMID IBN MOHAMMED BUT WAS BEST KNOWN AS **TIPPU-TIB** BY EUROPEANS. HE RULED EFFECTIVELY OVER HIS UNUSUALLY LARGE TRADING EMPIRE IN CENTRAL AFRICA, CONSISTING OF HIS RELATIVES AND ALLIES AS COMMERCIAL REPRESENTATIVES AT VARIOUS CENTRES. **TIB** WAS VERY RICH AND POWERFUL AND HAD INFLUENCE OVER MANY AFRICANS. HE DOMINATED CENTRAL AFRICA BEFORE THE REGION WAS SEIZED BY THE EUROPEANS. AFTER HIS DEATH, SOME GEOGRAPHICAL SOCIETIES IN EUROPE ACKNOWLEDGED HOW MUCH THEY WERE INDEBTED TO **TIPPU TIB** FOR ALLOWING EXPLORERS TO TRAVEL IN THE AREA WHERE HE WAS IN POWER AND COLLECT VALUABLE SCIENTIFIC DATA.

TRUGANINI

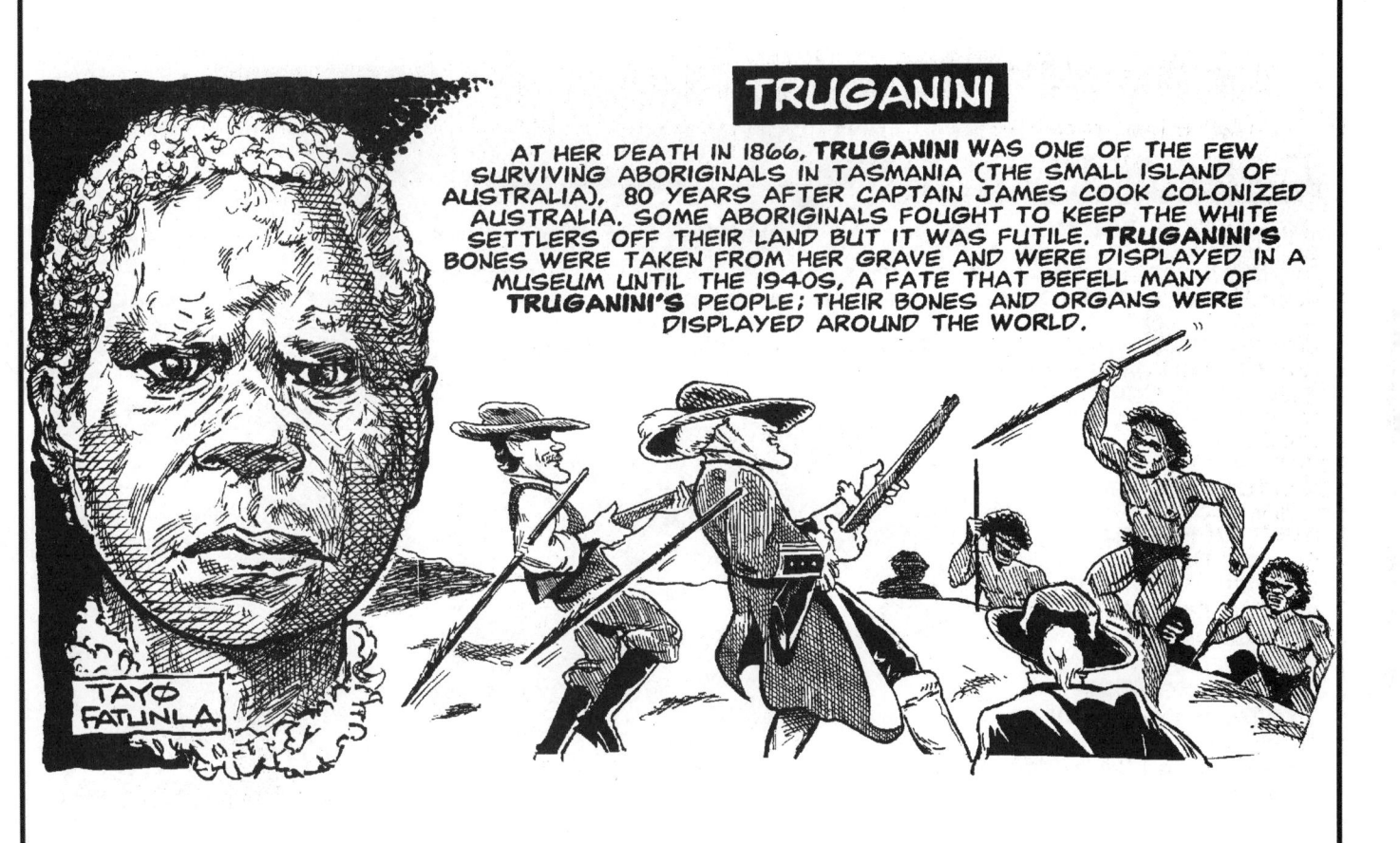

AT HER DEATH IN 1866, **TRUGANINI** WAS ONE OF THE FEW SURVIVING ABORIGINALS IN TASMANIA (THE SMALL ISLAND OF AUSTRALIA), 80 YEARS AFTER CAPTAIN JAMES COOK COLONIZED AUSTRALIA. SOME ABORIGINALS FOUGHT TO KEEP THE WHITE SETTLERS OFF THEIR LAND BUT IT WAS FUTILE. **TRUGANINI'S** BONES WERE TAKEN FROM HER GRAVE AND WERE DISPLAYED IN A MUSEUM UNTIL THE 1940S, A FATE THAT BEFELL MANY OF **TRUGANINI'S** PEOPLE; THEIR BONES AND ORGANS WERE DISPLAYED AROUND THE WORLD.

TAYO FATUNLA

SOJOURNER TRUTH

SOJOURNER TRUTH (1797-1883) WAS BORN ISABELLA BAUMFREE AS A SLAVE IN NEW YORK. FOR 40 YEARS, SHE SPENT HER LIFE TRAVELLING ALL OVER THE U.S. SPEAKING THE TRUTH ABOUT SLAVERY AND WOMEN'S RIGHTS, AND IN THE PROCESS SHE HELPED SHAKE OFF THE CHAINS OF SLAVERY.

SOJOURNER (WHICH MEANS "TRAVELLER") WAS CONSTANTLY ARRESTED AND BEATEN FOR SPEAKING OUT AGAINST SLAVERY BUT SHE KEPT ON WITH HER MISSION. THROUGH HER DEDICATION, **SOJOURNER** HELPED OPEN DOORS OF FREEDOM FOR ALL PEOPLE. THE "PATHFINDER" SPACE VEHICLE THAT LANDED ON MARS IN 1996 WAS OFFICIALLY NAMED AFTER **SOJOURNER TRUTH**, A NAME GIVEN BY 15-YEAR-OLD AFRICAN-AMERICAN VALERIE AMBROSE IN 1995.

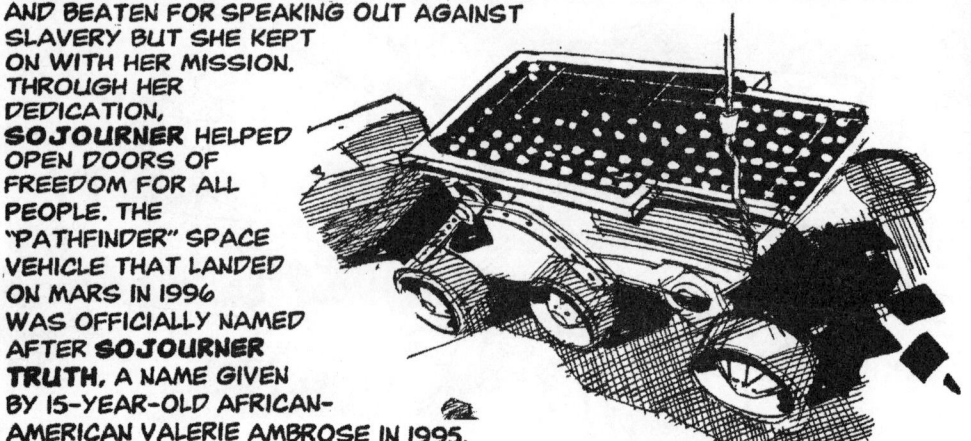

TAYO FATUNLA

TINA TURNER

SINGER **TINA TURNER** (1939-) WAS BORN BORN ANNA MAE BULLOCK IN TENNESSEE. AT THE AGE OF SEVENTEEN SHE MET IKE TURNER WHO WAS TO INVITE HER TO JOIN HIS BAND. THE CHEMISTRY WORKED AND THEY MARRIED, AND BOTH RECORDED THE HIT *LITTLE ANN* (1958) AND *A FOOL IN LOVE* (1960). IKE TURNER NAMED HIS BAND'S STAR LADY **TINA TURNER** DURING THEIR INTIMATE RELATIONSHIP. THEY WERE A SUCCESSFUL TOURING ACT IN THE 1960S BUT IN THE 1970S, **TURNER'S** RECORDS WERE NOT SELLING AND SHE DIVORCED IKE IN 1974. FAMOUS FOR HER DANCING AND MINI-SKIRTS TRADEMARKS, **TURNER'S** COMEBACK ALBUM (*PRIVATE DANCER*) IN 1984 WAS A MULTI-PLATINUM SELLING SUCCESS WHICH GAVE THE WORLD THE INTERNATIONALLY CHART TOPPING SINGLE, *WHAT'S LOVE GOT TO DO WITH IT*. A BIOGRAPHICAL MOVIE OF THE SAME TITLE WAS RELEASED IN 1993. ANGELA BASSETTE PLAYED THE ROLE OF **TINA TURNER**.

TAYO FATUNLA

SARAH VAUGHAN

SARAH VAUGHAN (1924-1990) WAS AN INTERNATIONALLY ACLAIMED AFRICAN-AMERICAN SINGER AND PIANIST. HER UNIQUE STYLE OF JAZZ WAS UNPARALLELED. AT THE AGE OF NINETEEN SHE ENTERED A CONTEST BY MAKING HER DEBUT AT HARLEM'S APOLLO THEATRE, NEW YORK IN 1943. BY 1950, **VAUGHAN** WAS AN INTERNATIONAL STAR TOURING OVER THE NEXT THREE DECADES. BORN IN NEWARK, NEW JERSEY, SHE RECORDED WITH JAZZ GREATS INCLUDING DIZZY GILLESPIE. **VAUGHAN** RECEIVED MANY AWARDS INCLUDING A GRAMMY IN 1983. HER NOTABLE SONGS INCLUDE *MY FUNNY VALENTINE* AND *RAINY DAYS*. IN HER LIVE PERFOMANCES, **SARAH VAUGHAN** NEVER SANG A SONG THE SAME WAY TWICE. SHE HAD A VOICE WITH THREE OCTAVES IN RANGE.

SHIRLEY VERRETT

Soprano singing actress **Shirley Verrett** (1931–) has featured at the world's great opera houses such as the Royal Opera House, Covent Garden in London, The Paris Opera (Theatre Des Champs Elysees) and the San Francisco Opera. Her opera debut was in New York in 1958 at the New York City Opera (Carnegie Hall). **Verrett** was born in New Orleans and began her career as a mezzo. She began singing in Europe from 1959. **Shirley Verrett** is a recipient of numerous honours and awards including the Marian Anderson Award and the Naumburg Award. She has played the roles of Lady Macbeth and Judith in her operatic performances.

DAVID WALKER

DAVID WALKER (1785-1830) IN HIS TIME WAS ONE OF THE MOST DYNAMIC BLACK ABOLITIONISTS IN AMERICA. BORN IN NORTH CAROLINA, **WALKER** SETTLED LATER IN LIFE IN BOSTON, MASSACHUSETTS WHERE HE OPENED A CLOTHING STORE. HE SPOKE WITHOUT FEAR ON THE SUBJECT OF ENDING SLAVERY. HE USED HIS MONEY FROM THE CLOTHING BUSINESS TO HELP OTHERS. WALKER PUBLISHED THE MOST POWERFUL PIECE OF ANTI-SLAVERY LITERATURE (*WALKER'S APPEAL*) AT THAT TIME. IT SHOOK UP THE NORTHERN ABOLITIONISTS AND HELPED TO ROUSE FREE BLACKS FROM THEIR GIVE-IN APPROACH TO SLAVERY AND INJUSTICE. **WALKER'S** APPEAL BOOK WAS BANNED BY SOUTHERN LEGISLATORS, HIS WORK WAS DENOUNCED BY OTHER ABOLITIONISTS AND MANY OF THE FREE BLACKS THOUGHT THAT IT WAS TOO RADICAL. THERE WAS A BOUNTY ON **WALKER'S** HEAD DEAD OR ALIVE NOT SURPRISINGLY, **DAVID WALKER** DIED MYSTERIOUSLY A YEAR LATER. HIS SPIRIT LIVED ON. MANY OTHER BLACKS WERE INFLUENCED BY WALKER'S APPEAL.

TAYO FATUNLA

DENZEL WASHINGTON

DENZEL WASHINGTON (1954–) WAS BORN IN MT. VERNON, NEW YORK. HE WAS PERHAPS THE MOST SUCCESSFUL AFRICAN-AMERICAN ACTOR OF THE EIGHTIES AND NINETIES IN MAINSTREAM FEATURE LENGTH MOVIES.
WASHINGTON'S CAREER STARTED OFF AT THE THEATRE. HE PLAYED DR. PHILLIP CHANDLER IN THE TELEVISION SERIES ST. ELSEWHERE.
WASHINGTON WENT ON TO FEATURE IN MINOR MOVIE ROLES AND THEN MAJOR ROLES IN MOVIES SUCH AS CRY FREEDOM (1980), GLORY (1989) MALCOLM X (1992), HURRICANE (2000), AND MISSISSIPPI MASALA (1992) TO MENTION A FEW. **DENZIL WASHINGTON** WON AND OSCAR FOR HIS SUPPORTING ROLE IN GLORY AND ANOTHER OSCAR FOR BEST ACTOR FOR HS ROLE IN TRAINING DAY (2002).

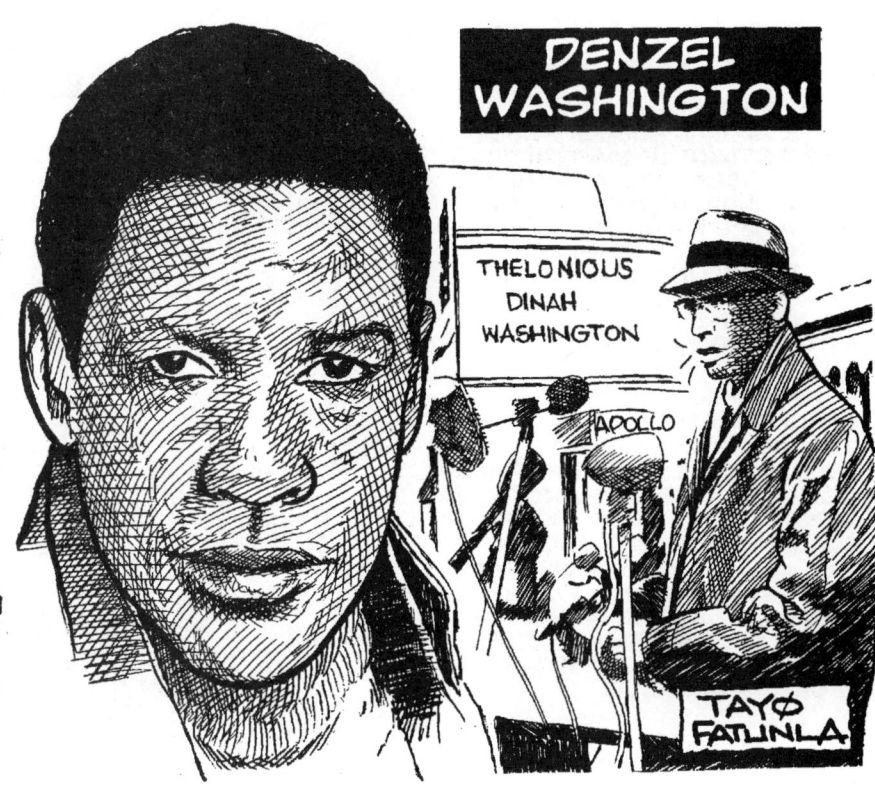

THELONIOUS DINAH WASHINGTON

APOLLO

TAYỌ FATUNLA

ARTHUR WHARTON

The world's first black professional soccer player was **Arthur Wharton** (1866-1930). Born in Accra, Gold Coast (now Ghana), in West Africa, **Wharton** was sent by his family to England to study, and it was while he was studying in Staffordshire that his athletic talents emerged. At the 1886 British AAA (Amateur Athletics Association) Championships, **Wharton** became the first man officially to run the old 100 yards in 10 seconds. In 1889, **Wharton** was signed by the elite British soccer club, Preston North End F.C., as a goalkeeper of great repute who also played other positions. Arthur **Wharton** was a sportsman who put black people on the world's sporting calendar.

TAYO FATUNLA

DOUGLAS WILDER

WHEN IN 1990 **DOUGLAS WILDER** (1931-) WAS ELECTED GOVERNOR OF THE STATE OF VIRGINIA, HE BECAME THE FIRST AFRICAN-AMERICAN TO BE POPULARLY ELECTED AS CHIEF EXECUTIVE OF ANY OF THE FIFTY STATES. **WILDER** FOUGHT IN THE KOREAN WAR (1952) AND WAS AWARDED A BRONZE STAR FOR HIS BRAVERY. HE WAS ALSO THE FIRST AFRICAN-AMERICAN STATE SENATOR (1969-85) AND LIEUTENANT GOVERNOR (1985). **DOUGLAS WILDER** HAS WON MANY AWARDS AND OWING TO HIS REMARKABLE SUCCESS, MANY BOOKS HAVE BEEN WRITTEN ABOUT HIM, INCLUDING *CLAIMING THE DREAM* (1990).

TAYO FATUNLA

BERT WILLIAMS

HE IS HARDLY KNOWN TODAY, BUT **BERT WILLIAMS** (1874-1922) WAS THE FIRST MAJOR BLACK STAR TO APPEAR IN FILMS AND STAR WITH WHITES IN A BIG TIME VAUDEVILLE SKETCH. **WILLIAMS** WAS BORN IN THE BAHAMAS. HE SETTLED IN THE U.S. AND PLAYED IN MINSTREL SHOWS. HE FEATURED IN FOUR BROADWAY SHOWS WITH GEORGE WALKER, DELIVERING SURPRISE PUNCH LINES AS "A DOWN TRODDEN DUPE". IN LONDON, **WILLIAMS** ALSO PLAYED A COMMAND PERFORMANCE AT BUCKINGHAM PALACE. HE WAS CONSIDERED ONE OF THE FINEST COMEDIANS IN HIS TIME. IN HIS SONGS *NOBODY* AND *THAT'S A PLENTY*, **WILLIAMS** CHALLENGED SOME STEREOTYPES.

BERT WILLIAMS STARED IN THE ZIEGFELD "FOLLIES" (1910-1919), THEREBY SHARING THE STAGE WITH W.C. FIELDS. OTHER SUCCESSES INCLUDE *ABYSSINIA* (1906) AND *MR LODE OF KOAL* (1909).

TAYO FATUNLA

DANIEL WILLIAMS

DR DANIEL HALE WILLIAMS (1856-1931) WAS THE FIRST DOCTOR TO EVER PERFORM OPEN HEART SURGERY (IN 1893). WILLIAMS' PATIENT LIVED FOR ANOTHER TWENTY YEARS. CRITICS CHALLENGED HIS MEDICAL KNOW-HOW, BUT IT DID NOT STOP HIM FROM IMPROVING THE PROFESSION. BORN IN PENNSYLVANIA IN 1913, WILLIAMS BECAME THE FIRST AFRICAN-AMERICAN MEMBER OF THE AMERICAN COLLEGE OF SURGEONS.

TAYO FATUNLA

ERIC WILLIAMS

DR **ERIC WILLIAMS** (1911-1981) WAS BORN IN PORT-OF-SPAIN IN TRINIDAD. CONVINCED OF THE NEED FOR ORGANIZED POLITICS IN THE CARIBBEAN, IN 1956 **WILLIAMS** LAUNCHED THE MASSES PARTY, THE PEOPLE'S NATIONAL MOVEMENT; HIS ONE-MAN CRUSADE RESULTED IN VICTORY FOR THE PARTY IN THE GENERAL ELECTION THAT SAME YEAR WHEN TRINIDAD AND TOBAGO BECAME INTERNALLY SELF-GOVERNING. **WILLIAMS** BECAME THE COUNTRY'S FIRST PRIME MINISTER, SERVING FROM 1961 TO 1981. HE LED HIS COUNTRY TO INDEPENDENCE IN 1962. **ERIC WILLIAMS** WAS THE AUTHOR OF MANY BOOKS INCLUDING CAPITALISM AND SLAVERY.

STEPHEN WILTSHIRE

THE CHILD ARTIST **STEPHEN WILTSHIRE** (1987-) HAS THE AMAZING ABILITY TO CAPTURE PERSPECTIVE AND MOOD THROUGH HIS SKETCHES AND, IN PARTICULAR, BUILDINGS WITH EXTRAORDINARY ACCURACY. SUFFERING FROM AUTISM, **WILTSHIRE** AT THE AGE OF TWELVE CAME TO THE ATTENTION OF THE PUBLIC IN A TELEVISION DOCUMENTARY ABOUT HIS DRAWING SKILLS. THIS TRANSFORMED HIS WORLD, BY HIGHLIGHTING **WILTSHIRE'S** DISABILITIES AND REMARKABLE CREATIVE ARTISTIC SKILLS. HE WAS DESCRIBED AT THAT AGE AS "POSSIBLY THE BEST CHILD ARTIST IN BRITAIN". **WILTSHIRE'S** ABILITY TO LOOK AT A BUILDING FOR A WHILE AND REPRODUCE IT FROM MEMORY IS REMARKABLE AND HE CAN REPRODUCE FROM A PHOTOGRAPH AND DRAW IMAGINATIVE BUILDINGS. **STEPHEN WILTSHIRE** ALSO HAS AN EXTENSIVE KNOWLEDGE OF AUTOMOBILES AND HISTORY OF EARTHQUAKES. CITIES **WILTSHIRE** HAS BEEN TO AND HAS DRAWN INCLUDE NEW YORK, PARIS AND MOSCOW.

TAYO FATUNLA

OPRAH WINFREY

"EXCELLENCE IS THE BEST DETERRENT TO RACISM OR SEXISM..." THESE ARE THE WORDS OF **OPRAH WINFREY** (1954-), THE FIRST WOMAN IN HISTORY TO OWN AND PRODUCE HER OWN TV TALK SHOW, THE OPRAH WINFREY SHOW. **OPRAH** WAS BORN IN MISSISSIPPI AND SHE WON AN ACADEMY AWARD NOMINATION FOR HER ROLE IN *THE COLOR PURPLE* IN 1986. **OPRAH'S** SHOW BEGAN SYNDICATION IN 1986 AND THE CHANGES IN HER TALK SHOW HAVE BEEN PART OF THE AMERICAN CULTURE AND HAVE SHAPED MANY LIVES ALL OVER THE WORLD.

RICHARD WRIGHT

JAMES BALDWIN WAS INSPIRED BY **RICHARD WRIGHT** (1908-1960) TO BECOME A WRITER. **WRIGHT** WAS A POWERFUL WRITER WHO DEPICTED THE EFFECTS OF RACIAL SEGREGATION ON AFRICAN-AMERICANS. HE GAINED IMMEDIATE FAME WHEN HIS NOVEL *NATIVE SON* SET IN A CHICAGO GHETTO, WAS PUBLISHED IN 1940. HE WAS BORN IN MISSISSIPPI. **WRIGHT'S** OTHER BOOKS INCLUDE *UNCLE TOM'S CHILDREN* (FOUR NOVELLAS DRAWING ON HIS YOUTH IN MISSISSIPPI). THE BOOK EARNED **WRIGHT** POPULARITY INTERNATIONALLY, WINNING HIM AN AWARD FOR THE BEST PIECE OF FICTION PUBLISHED BY WPA AND A GUGGENHEIM FELLOWSHIP. *BLACK BOY* (1945) AND *THE OUTSIDERS* WERE ALSO SUCCESSFUL PUBLICATIONS BY **RICHARD WRIGHT** WHO DIED LATER IN LIFE IN PARIS.

BENJAMIN ZEPHANIAH

Dreadlocked poet, writer and performer **Benjamin Iqbal Zephaniah** (1958-) was born in Birmingham, England. He did not have a pleasant childhood but performed his sometimes political, funny, critical and social poems to the delight of people. **Zephaniah** would perform on pavements and in town halls, community centres and at times churches. Fame took **Zephaniah** by surprise after he won a poetry competition. He became in demand, performing with lots of movements. Internationally, he became well known, listened to by millions. **Zephaniah** was asked to be a poet in residence at both Oxford and Cambridge universities. In the year 2003, **Benjamin Zephaniah** refused to be honoured with *Order of the British Empire* (OBE) by Her Majesty the Queen.

TAYO FATUNLA

MOHAMMED OULD ZUM ZUM

Born in Char, Mauritania in West Africa **MOHAMMED OULD ZUM ZUM** was an exceptional guide in the world's largest desert, the Sahara Desert, in the northern region of Africa. The desert covers 9 million square kilometres, an area the size of America. **MOHAMMED OULD ZUM ZUM** was blind from birth, yet he was able to lead caravans all over the desert.

TAYO FATUNLA

Twenty Questions

1) In which country is Paul Bogle a National Hero?
2) Who was known as the Queen of Mambo and Salsa music?
3) The Aborigines are natives of which country?
4) What was the famous vessel used to transport the first mass migration from Jamaica to Britain known as?
5) He made the whole world pay attention to "Bollywood". Who was he?
6) Who was the brave nurse on the battlefields of the Crimean war?
7) In which country is the statue of Christ the Redeemer a tourist attraction?
8) Pan Africanist Julius Nyerere was leader of which country?
9) Who said "excellence is the best deterent to racism and sexism"?
10) Where did the process of embalming originate?
11) Tom Adams was Prime Minister of which Caribbean Island?
12) Who led a victorious march to Alabama? Dr. Martin Luther King or Malcolm X ?
13) Where is the holiest shrine of Islam, the Kaaba?
14) Dr. Nnamdi Azikiwe was the first president of which independent country?
15) Who was the first doctor to perform open heart surgery?
16) Of which Kingdom was Yaa Asantewa a famous fighter?
17) What are tribal marks?
18) George Milwa Pemba was an early artist of which country?
19) Who is Britain's first black television newscaster?
20) What region did the Mayas occupy?